WHY INDIANA
IS THE CENTER OF THE
BASKETBALL WORLD

Michael G. Ludlow

authorHOUSE®

AuthorHouse™
1663 Liberty Drive
Bloomington, IN 47403
www.authorhouse.com
Phone: 1 (800) 839-8640

Published by AuthorHouse 11/29/2017

ISBN: 978-1-5462-1798-5 (sc)
ISBN: 978-1-5462-1799-2 (e)

Table of Contents

Introduction

In 1925 James Naismith visited an Indiana basketball state finals game and later wrote "Basketball really had its origin in Indiana, which remains the center of the sport."[1]

Indiana has long been known to be basketball crazy. The image of a basketball goal on every garage, barn or any other place you can put one (including the governor's residence) is based, as most legends are, on a ring of truth. Indiana has always been basketball crazy. Decades before "March Madness" became a national trademark, *Hoosier Hysteria* rippled through the entire state at tourney time.

The following is a result of over 3000 hours of research into the origins of the contributions Hoosiers have made to basketball that has helped make it the 2nd most popular game in the world in the number of participants, fans, and leagues.

Merriam-Webster's on-line dictionary defines center as:

a: a point, ***area***, person, or thing that is most important or pivotal in relation to an indicated activity, interest, or condition

b: a ***source*** from which something **originates**

This document analyzes Hoosier's contributions to the way basketball is played, coached, administered, promoted, and enjoyed. The analysis is organized as follows:

- Players
- Coaches
- Innovators/ Contributors
- Additional Supporting Facts
- Interesting Trivia

I contend that the evidence presented herein provides an overwhelming case for

Why Indiana is the Center of the Basketball World.

---

[1] http://en.wikipedia.org/wiki/Indiana

About the Author

I played high school basketball at Carmel (67/68 and 68/69) and freshman basketball at a D3 school. But my most memorable basketball "achievement" came in the 1964 Hamilton County Junior High School tournament. As the lone 7th grader on the team, I only played when the outcome was determined.

In one game with about a minute to go we fouled one of their players. Before he could take his free throws, both coaches emptied their benches. Nine new players took their positions along the lane. I had always taken the inside position on the 7th grade team, but was "displaced" to the 3rd position by a bigger 8th grader.

The free throw attempt hit the back of the rim and came out to me. Grabbing the rebound in an outside position, my instincts took over and I immediately turned facing the basket, head faked the defenseman into the air, and got clobbered taking my shot.

We lined up for another free throw attempt with me at the line. When the ref handed me the ball, the horn sounded. He took the ball from me and both refs went to the scorer's table. The refs and the scoring table started laughing. A discussion followed before the refs came back onto the floor and waved us down to the opposite basket.

I had shot at the wrong basket and the officials had to determine whether I got to shoot the frows. They decided that, since the basket would have counted had it gone in, it was a shot, I got fouled, therefore, I get to shoot the free throws.

As we walked to the other end and everyone realized what had happened, the entire gym was laughing: except me and the guy who fouled me. Had I made the shot, I would have been the first (and probably only) person in the history of Hamilton County basketball to be in both teams' box scores.

Why Indiana is the Center of the Basketball World

Did You Know?

1. Indiana has the highest concentration of coaches in NCAA Division I history
2. Indiana has the highest concentration of consensus All-Americans in NCAA Division I history
3. Indiana has the highest concentration of players in NBA history
4. Indiana has the highest concentration of coaches in NBA history
5. The six largest and thirteen of the fourteen largest high school gymnasiums are in Indiana
6. An Indiana high school is the most famous high school basketball team in history
7. A Hoosier was selected as the best coach of any sport
8. A Hoosier invented the orange basketball
9. A Hoosier developed the fast break style of basketball
10. A Hoosier developed the recruiting process used by college coaches today
11. A Hoosier developed the first basketball shoe
12. In 1919 a Hoosier developed the intramural system that is used today
13. Hoosiers are largely responsible for developing the ACC into the basketball power it is today
14. A Hoosier is the most successful coach in NCAA Tournament history
15. A Hoosier is the only person to lead the NCAA in scoring AND win the NCAA Championship in the same year
16. A Hoosier developed the first basketball clinic
17. A Hoosier is largely responsible for free agency in the NBA
18. A Hoosier is largely responsible for expanding the NBA's salary cap rules
19. A Hoosier was the first person inducted into the Naismith Basketball Hall of Fame as a player and a coach
20. A Hoosier was the first Executive Director of the Naismith Hall of Fame
21. A Hoosier is the ABA's career leader in points and assists
22. A Hoosier is responsible for establishing the post season conference tournament winner getting the automatic bid to the NCAA tournament
23. Two of the first five people voted into the 1st class of the College Basketball Hall of Fame are Hoosiers
24. Three of the first nine people inducted as Players into the Naismith Hall of Fame are from Indiana
25. The "epitome of cool" played high school basketball in Indiana
26. Indiana is the only state with a population under 10 million to have at least three persons playing in every NBA season.
27. A Hoosier was the first coach to recruit an African-American in the Big Ten
28. A Hoosier is the only player to win NBA championships with both the Lakers and the Celtics
29. The University of Minnesota missed two opportunities to hire Hall of Fame "Indiana" coaches
30. A Hoosier was the first coach to film his games
31. One of the most venerated ACC basketball arenas is named for a Culver graduate.
32. Indiana has the only state-wide high school basketball Hall of Fame
33. A Hoosier is responsible for the use of an official time clock
34. *Hoosiers* is the consensus best movie ever made about basketball
35. Dr. James Naismith called Indiana "the center of basketball"
36. The coach of Ball State's only win against IU was an IU Hall of Famer
37. The only coach to be undefeated in the NCAA Tournament is a Hoosier
38. The only person in the history of the NBA to be Player of the Year, Coach of the Year, and Executive of the year is a Hoosier
39. The Indiana Pacers are the only ABA team absorbed by the NBA to play all nine ABA seasons
40. A Hoosier is responsible for the establishment of the 10 second line
41. A Hoosier is the only man selected as an NCAA Basketball All-American for two schools

Measuring Source of Players and Coaches

The premise for this analysis is that a person's "source" is the primary state where their skills were developed, i.e., high school. The best hone their skills in college (sometimes), and the best of the best apply them at the highest level of the game, professional basketball.

This study measures the strength of each State as a source of players and coaches by *Concentration* [Con] and is calculated as the number of persons from a state per million of the population of the state.

States with very low populations can produce very high concentrations with very few persons. Twelve states (including DC) have populations less than 1 million. These states are considered outliers and are not considered as participants in the analysis. Because of the statistical insignificance of the population of DC, the population and players from DC are divided equally between Virginia and Maryland.

Players

This study measured each state's concentration of players in the NBA, ABA, NCAA All-Americans, and Naismith Hall of Famers.

NBA

4141 persons have played in at least one game in the NBA from 1946-47 (BAA) through the 2016-17 season. The source of three hundred and thirteen (313) of these (7.00%) is outside of the United States. Table SO-1 displays the concentrations of players entering the league from each state in each decade and for all years.

California (CA), New York (NY) and Illinois (IL) have provided the most players to the NBA with 442, 375, and 257, respectively. They also have the 1st, 3rd, and 5th highest populations.

The 172 NBAers from Indiana (IN) computes to a Concentration of 33.403, the highest for any state. Kentucky's (KY) 98 players results in the 2nd highest Concentration (27.930/million); Mississippi (MS) with 68 players has the 3rd highest (27.527/million); Maryland (MD) has the 4th highest (27.420/million) with a total of 118 players; and Louisiana (LA) with 91 players has the 5th highest Concentration of 24.738.

Indiana is the only state with Concentrations of new players in the top 15 for each decade. Indiana's concentrations have declined since the 1980's as the rest of the country began to catch up to the realization of the greatness of basketball. Maryland has had the first or second highest concentration for each decade beginning with the 80's. Mississippi has also been a consistent producer since the 70's. Since 2010, Indiana has provided the highest concentration of players.

Longevity: Number of Games Played

Table SO-2 displays each state's concentration of NBA players by ranges of games played [GP]. 2326 of the 3828 US born players have played at least 100 games. Indiana is the only state with concentrations in the top three for all ranges of games up to 700.

Of the 972 players who have played at least 500 games (a minimum of 6.7 seasons at 75 games per season), Indiana has the highest concentration. For the 748 players who played at least 600 games (a minimum of 8 seasons at 75 games per season), Indiana has the second highest concentration.

Consistency of States as a Source of NBA Players

Another measure of the strength of a state as a source of NBA players is its consistency for producing players. There have been 71 NBA seasons through the 2016-17 season. Indiana is one of only nine states to have produced at least one player in every NBA season.

ABA

517 persons played at least one minute in the 9 seasons (67/68 through (75/76) of the American Basketball Association (ABA).[2] Of the 517 players, 206 (39.85%) played in the NBA.

Table SO-3 shows that New York, Pennsylvania and California provided the most players to the ABA with 53, 52, and 44, respectively. They also had the 2nd, 3rd, and 1st highest populations in the 70's, respectively.

Indiana (IN) had the 4th most number of players (37) which computed to the 2nd highest concentration (6.925) behind only Kentucky (30) players and an 8.718 concentration.

Indiana players made significant contributions to the league's play.

- Louie Dampier is the career leader in games played, minutes played, points, assists, and three point field goals.

- Don Buse is the career leader in steals; George McGinnis is 9th.

- Five of the top eleven career assist/turnover ratios are from Hoosiers: Buse (1st), Billy Shepherd (3rd), Dampier (6th), Billy Keller (10th), and John Barnhill (11th).

- Four of the top ten three point field goal percentages are by Hoosiers: Keller (5th), Shepherd (6th), Jimmy Rayl (9th) and Keller (10th).

- Billy Shepherd holds the single season three point goal shooting percentage.

- Slick Leonard was selected as the best ABA coach

---

[2] I did not include Penny Ann Early, the only woman to ever play in a professional basketball game, because she played 1 second in a November 28, 1968, game for the Kentucky Colonels against the Los Angeles Stars as a publicity stunt. She was the first licensed female jockey and every male rider boycotted the first three races she rode in so the Kentucky Colonels owner decided to have her on the team as a show of support for her as an athlete. She entered the game during a timeout, inbounded the ball to a teammate who immediately called timeout and she was replaced. She had never played basketball in college or high school.
http://www.remembertheaba.com/onlyintheabamaterial/onlyintheaba4.html

NCAA All-Americans

This study measured the concentrations of the number of All-American selections and the number of players selected for every year (1905 – 2017). Table SO-4 displays the results of these calculations. I could not find the "state" for fifty-five of the players selected all of whom were selected before 1929.

Indiana has the highest concentrations of All-American Selections (26.949/million) and Number of Players (17.801/million), more than 9 and 5.5 per million more than the 2nd highest concentrations, respectively.

Of the states with the ten highest concentrations all time only Maryland, North Carolina, Oklahoma, and Oregon have less than 50% of their selections before 1970 with Oregon and Oklahoma having 47.7% and 41.7% of their selections before 1970, respectively.

Maryland, North Carolina, New York, and Oregon have less than 50% of their players selected before 1970 with Oregon and New York having 47.7% and 48.3% of their selections before 1970, respectively.

Indiana is the only state with one of the ten highest concentrations of selections for each period measured and one of the five highest concentrations for each period except the 1980-1989 decade. It is also the only state with one of the eleven highest concentrations of players selected for each period measured.

An interesting fact is that Hoosier Elmer Oliphant is the only person to be selected at two different schools. He was selected in 1914 while playing for Purdue and for Army in 1914/15.

An even more interesting fact is that basketball was possibly his third best sport.

Elmer Oliphant

Elmer "Ollie" Oliphant was born in Bloomfield, IN, July 9, 1892. He attended Linton High School, working part-time in the local coal mines. He lettered in football, basketball, baseball, and captained the track team to the 1910 State Championship. He also worked part-time and summers in the local coal mines which helped develop 174 pounds of muscle onto his 5'7" frame.

He went to Purdue without a scholarship and graduated with a degree in mechanical engineering and seven letters in football, basketball, baseball, and track. He was a prolific scorer in football as a runner and kicker and still holds the Purdue single game scoring record with 43 points.

Upon graduation he accepted an appointed to West Point where he continued to be a scoring machine setting the Army single season record (125) as well as the single game record (45) he still holds today. He earned four varsity letters in baseball, three in football, three in basketball, and one in track and field creating the need for a specially designed "letter" that is still the only one ever made.

While at West Point he also set the world record for the 220 yard low hurdles on grass and played hockey, swam, and boxed and was Champion Boxer in the Corps of Cadets. While in military service at West Point in 1919, he invented the intramural sports system as we know it today.[3]

---

[3] http://www4.lib.purdue.edu/archon/?p=creators/creator&id=682

Why Indiana is the Center of the Basketball World

He played two years in the forerunner of the NFL, the American Professional Football Association (APFA) and led the league in scoring in its final year.

The following synopsis of his athletic accomplishments provides an overwhelming case for Ollie Oliphant being the finest all-around athlete to come from Indiana.

- Two time consensus All-American in basketball (1914, 1915)
- Two time All-American in football (1916,1917)
- 220 yard low hurdle world record
- Eighteen Letters across four sports in college
- Army Athletic Association Trophy (1918)
- Helms Athletic Foundation Hall of Fame (1953)
- Indiana Football Hall of Fame in (1975)
- Purdue Athletics Hall of Fame (1997)
- Kappa Sigma Fraternity Hall of Fame (1997)
- Army Sports Hall of Fame (2004)
- Football Writers Association of America All-time All-America Team for players before 1919
- Yost All-time All-America Team
- Indiana Basketball Hall of Fame (2012)

Hall of Fame

There are 184 persons inducted into the Naismith Memorial Hall of Fame as players. Table SO-HOF shows the Concentration of Hall of Fame players by State. Indiana and New York have virtually the same concentrations of players (1.748 and 1.741, respectively) with Kentucky (1.710) a very close third.

John Wooden

John Wooden was born October 14, 1910, near Martinsville, IN. He is world renown for being one of (if not the) best basketball coach in history. Before he became a coach he was an incredible basketball player. He led his Martinsville high school to three consecutive Final Games in the state tournament (1926, '27 and '28) winning the title in 1927. He lost to future Purdue teammate Stretch Murphy's Marion Giants in '26 and to Muncie Central in 1928 when Bearcats center Charlie Secrest grabbed his own center jump tip with time running out, turned and fired a shot from mid-court that went in for a 13-12 victory, avenging their loss to Martinsville in the final game of the preceding year.

Wooden continued his winning ways at Purdue where he was a three time consensus All-American. He was College Basketball Player of the Year his senior year as well as being on Purdue's only National Championship, all three as selected by the then ruling body of college basketball – the Helms Athletic Foundation.

His relentless determination was evidenced by the nicknames given to him as the "Human Floor Burn" and the "Indiana Rubber Man" for the way he, literally, threw himself into the game and the quick way he recovered to stay in the play. He ended his career as the Big Ten's all-time leading scorer. His intelligence was acknowledged with the Big Ten Medal of Honor received his senior year for having the highest GPA of all Big Ten basketball players.

He played professionally in the forerunner of the NBA, the NBL (National Basketball League) for nine seasons primarily for the Indianapolis Kautskys, so named for their owner – Frank Kautsky. He played 30-40 games per year at a salary of $50 per game while coaching high school. He led the league in scoring his first year and in one stretch hit 134 consecutive free throws. When he hit his 100th straight free throw, Kautsky stopped the game and presented him a $100 bill, the first he had ever seen.

He was inducted into Indiana Basketball Hall of Fame in 1962 and the Naismith Memorial Basketball Hall of Fame as a player in 1960.

Synopsis of John's Career Accomplishments as a Player:

- Played in three consecutive Indiana State Championship games, 1926, 1927, & 1928
- Indiana State Champion, 1927
- Helms Athletic Foundation All-America at Purdue University, 1930, 1931, 1932
- Helms Athletic Foundation Player of the Year, 1932
- National championship with Purdue University, 1932
- Graduated as Big Ten's all-time leading scorer
- Big Ten Medal of Honor for highest GPA of all basketball players, 1932
- All-NBL First Team, 1938

Branch McCracken

Emmitt Branch McCracken was born June 9, 1908, in Monrovia, IN. He is known primarily for his tenure as IU coach, winning two NCAA Championships, and for implementing the style that earned IU the nickname "Hurrying Hoosiers." Branch was a phenomenal player in high school and college. In high school he played at Monrovia during the time John Wooden played at nearby Martinsville thwarting his chance to go past the Sectionals. He had to settle for twice being named the MVP in the 74 team Tri-State Tournament held in Cincinnati leading Monrovia to the championship in 1925 and 1926. Monrovia had a total of 32 male students at that time.

One of Everett Dean's earliest recruits at IU was Branch "Big Bear" McCracken in 1926. He earned the nickname "Big Bear" because of his size (6' 4"), the intensity with which he played the game and the constant glower he wore while playing. McCracken led Indiana in scoring for three straight years, 1928-30, setting the Big Ten season scoring record in 1930 with 147 points. He was All Big Ten first Team all three of his seasons at IU, Big Ten MVP in 1928 and was selected as a Helm's All-American in 1930.

Branch began his coaching career at Ball State in 1930. He coached for nine seasons while playing professionally for Indianapolis, Fort Wayne, Dayton, Ohio, and in Oshkosh, Wis. He compiled a 93-41 record (69.4%) including what is still the school's only win over IU. When Dean left for Stanford in 1938, McCracken continued Dean's tradition of fast break basketball.

In 1940, IU finished 2nd in the Big Ten at 9-3 to Piggy Lambert's Purdue Boilermakers. IU had defeated Purdue twice; but they were Purdue's only losses. Lambert was public about his lack of respect for all postseason tournaments so the conference selected IU to represent it, technically because IU had won both meetings against the Boilers. McCracken's fast break style stunned fans and the media while blitzing Kansas by eighteen points for the championship. The Associated Press reported that IU shot "an amazing .333" and IU's nickname as the "Hurryin' Hoosiers" was born.

McCracken coached through the 64/65 season missing the 43/44 through 45/46 seasons to serve as a lieutenant in the Navy during World War II. He compiled a 364-174 overall record (67.7%) and a 210-116 Big Ten conference record (64.4%). He won a 2nd NCAA Championship in 1953. His IU teams made four NCAA Tournament appearances. He was selected the Coach of the Year in 1940 and 1953. In 1948, McCracken was responsible for recruiting Bill Garrett who became the first African American player in Big Ten basketball history.

He was one of the first eight players inducted into the Naismith Memorial Basketball Hall of Fame in 1960. He entered the Indiana Basketball Hall of Fame in 1963. He died five days before his 62nd birthday, June, 4, 1970. The floor at Assembly Hall in Bloomington is named for him as is the gymnasium at Monrovia.

Synopsis of Branch's Career Accomplishments:

- Tri-State Tournament Championship, 1925, 1926
- Tri-State Tournament MVP, 1925, 1926
- Led IU in scoring for three straight years, 1928-30
- All-Big Ten First Team, 1928-30
- Set the Big Ten record of 147 points, 1930
- Helms Foundation All-America, 1930
- Coach of the Year 1940, 1953
- IU floor at Assembly Hall named for McCracken

Stretch Murphy

Charles "Stretch" Murphy was born April 10, 1907, in Marion, Indiana. He is considered to be "one of basketball's first great big men."[4] At 6' 6" he was a mammoth for his time. He combined this size with agility and quickness which enabled him to dominate both in high school and college. His Marion Giants defeated John Wooden's Martinsville team in the state finals to win the 1926 Indiana state championship.

He was the prototype of the big man for Piggy Lambert's system at Purdue where he became a three time All-American for the Boilermakers. His defensive prowess and his ability to grab a defensive rebound and make a quick outlet pass enabled Lambert to perfect his fast break style of basketball, completely changing the way the game was played. He set the Big Ten scoring record his junior year with 143 points and led the Boilers his senior year to an undefeated Big Ten season along with sophomore sensation, John Wooden. Wooden would later say of Stretch, "There is no doubt that it was Murphy who started me on my way to being an outstanding player. I might not have become so well known if I hadn't played with him as a sophomore."[5]

Murphy and Wooden along with fellow Hoosier and IU star Branch McCracken were three of the six consensus All-Americans in 1930.

After graduating from Purdue, Murphy played for the American Basketball League's Chicago Bruins and the independent Indianapolis Kautskys. He coached at Edinburgh for a few years before becoming a major contributor to the development of Boy's Clubs. His work at the Bristol, CT, Boy's Club garnered him national recognition. He finished his career as Executive Director of the Tampa, FL, Boy's Club.

He was inducted into the Naismith Memorial Basketball Hall of Fame in 1960 and into the Indiana Basketball Hall of Fame in 1963. He died in August, 1992

Synopsis of Stretch's Career Accomplishments:

- Indiana High School Championship 1926
- Big Ten co-championships at Purdue 1928, 1929
- Helms Foundation All-America 1929, 1930
- Set Big Ten scoring record of 143 points 1929
- Big Ten Championship 1930

---

[4] http://www.hoophall.com/hall-of-famers/tag/charles-c-murphy
[5] *They Call Me Coach,* by John Wooden and Jack Tobin, p.54, published by McGraw-Hill

Robert "Fuzzy" Vandivier

Fuzzy Vandivier was born in Franklin, IN, December 26, 1903. He grew up playing basketball with friends Burl Friddle, Johnny "Snake Eyes" Gant, Ralph Hicks, Paul White, Sima Comer, Harold Borden, and Pete Keeling. By the time they got to high school, they knew each other so well that under coach, Ernest "Griz" Wagner, they dominated Indiana high school basketball winning the state championship three consecutive years, 1920, '21, and '22, going 29-1, 29-4 and 31-4, respectively, for small Franklin High School earning them the nickname "The Wonder Five."[6] They had winning streaks of 29 and 48 consecutive games during that stretch.

Fuzzy was the captain and the most prominent member of the team making All-State all three of their championship seasons. John Wooden, Oscar Robertson and George McGinnis are the only other Hoosiers so honored. Wooden called Fuzzy "the greatest high school basketball player of all time."[7] He was an outstanding offensive player with an accurate outside shot and incredible passing skills.

Upon graduation the entire team, including coach Wagner, continued to play together at home at Franklin College. They continued their winning ways going undefeated and winning the national championship in 1923. They took on all comers including Illinois, Purdue, Wisconsin and Notre Dame. They even played the Detroit Omars, a professional team, twice and beat them both times.

Fuzzy captained Franklin for two seasons and was an All-Midwest College All-Star in 1926. A serious injury to his back forced him to retire from playing during his senior year. The Chicago Tribune named him one of the five best players in the nation[8] in 1924. Upon graduation he returned to Franklin High school as head coach from 1926 to 1944. His teams won 14 Sectionals, 3 Regionals, and went to the Final Game in 1939 where they were defeated by Everett Case's Frankfort Hot Dogs. He died July 30, 1983.

He was inducted into the Indiana Basketball Hall of Fame in 1962 and into the Naismith Memorial Basketball Hall of Fame in 1975.

Synopsis of Fuzzy's Career Accomplishments:

- Three time State champion, 1920, 1921, 1922
- All-State 1920, 1921, 1922
- Captain of The Wonder Five
- Undefeated National Champion, 1923
- All Mid-West, 1926

---

[6] See The chapter The "Franklin Wonder Five" in the *Most Famous High school Teams* section below for details
[7] http://en.wikipedia.org/wiki/Fuzzy_Vanndivier
[8] Ibid.

Oscar Robertson

Oscar Robertson was born November 28, 1938, in Charlotte, Tennessee, and grew up in Indianapolis. At Crispus Attucks Ray Crowe, younger brother of Indiana's first Mr. Basketball, drilled the fundamentals of the game into Oscar making him a complete basketball player: scorer, rebounder, defensive stopper, and most importantly, making his teammates better.

"All I was ever thinking about was trying to do whatever I could to put my teammates into a position where I could get the maximum amount of production out of them and me. The idea, I always thought, was to get the weakest offensive player into the game and playing above his average. If you have a guy who usually gets two points and you can raise him up to 10 or 12, that's how you win."[9]

His sophomore year (1954) they were defeated in the afternoon of the Finals by Milan's miracle run to the Championship. Attucks won back to back state championships in 1955 and 1956, the '56 team being Indiana's first undefeated state champion and Oscar was selected as Mr. Basketball.

In his three years at Cincinnati he led the Bearcats to a 79-9 record (89.8%) and two Final Fours. In each of his three years he led the NCAA in scoring, was named 1st Team All-American, and chosen as College Player of the Year. When he graduated, he was the all-time leading NCAA scorer and held fourteen NCAA records.

He continued his dominance in the NBA with the Cincinnati Royals. Oscar was the first "big guard." A 6-5, 200 pound point guard, Oscar could jump over anyone his size and his quickness enabled him to drive around bigger opponents. All NBA defensive player Wali Jones described how he guarded Oscar. "I would pick up Oscar from the locker room and stick to him on every inch of the court. The refs would allow me to beat on him. Mendy Rudolph would not let me beat on Gail Goodrich or Jerry West like that. But it was OK on Oscar. I beat on him and I beat on him and if he finished with 30 points, I figured I did a good job."[10]

Attaining a "Triple-Double," double digit totals in three statistics usually points, assists and rebounds is a rare occurrence and is the lead highlight ESPN features when reporting on the outcome of an NBA game, often the lead of an entire broadcast. The less monumental but still very significant accomplishment by an NBA player is the attainment of a "Double-Double" which is always included in the recap of a game. The total number of Triple-Doubles and Double-Doubles a player has in a season is reported as well.

To average a Double-Double for an entire season is extremely rare. The rarity of this accomplishment is measured by the fact that in the history of the NBA, in the 20,690 seasons by players that have played at least 40 games in a season, only 252 players have averaged a double-double for an entire regular season (8.5%). 221 players averaged doubles in points and rebounds; 33 players averaged doubles in points and assists.

The players who averaged a double-double in points and rebounds did so 836 times. Charles Barkley did it 15 times. Wilt and Moses Malone had 14 seasons; Shaq, Tim Duncan, and Dwight Howard 13 times each. A total of 19 players did it ten or more times. More than half of the players who did average a double-double did so only once (70 players) or twice (41 players).

---

[9] *"Big O: An all-around talent like the league has never seen"*, Fran Blinebury, NBA.com Mar 12, 2012, at http://www.nba.com/2012/history/features/03/12/season-of-giants-oscar-robertson/
[10] ibid

Why Indiana is the Center of the Basketball World

Only thirty-three players have averaged double digit points and assists for a season. Nineteen of these players did it only once and one other only twice. John Stockton has the most with 10 seasons of double digit points and assists; Magic Johnson did it nine times.

Only two people, Oscar Robertson and Russell Westbrook, have averaged a triple-double for an entire season. In the 1961/62 season Oscar averaged 30.78 points, 11.38 assists and 12.47 rebounds. Westbrook did it in the 2016/17 season averaging 31.6 points, 10.7 rebounds and 10.4 assists. Oscar averaged a triple-double for his first five seasons (60/61 through 64/65) with 30.26 points, 10.61 assists and 10.40 rebounds.

The magnitude of this accomplishment is demonstrated by the fact that only six players have even come close to averaging a Triple-Double for a season. 'Close' is defined as at least a Double-Double and at least 7.5 in another stat. Wilt Chamberlain did it twice: averaging 24.16 points, 7.78 assists and 24.15 rebounds in the 66/67 season and averaging 24.29 points, 8.56 assists and 23.80 rebounds in the 67/68 season.

Magic Johnson came close twice averaging 16.78 points, 10.49 assists and 8.65 rebounds in the 82/83 season; and 22.47 points, 12.83 assists and 7.88 rebounds in the 88/89 season. Jason Kidd came close in the 2007/08 season averaging 10.80 points, 10.08 assists and 7.53 rebounds. And most recently, Russell Westbrook came close in the 2015/16 season with 23.48 points 7.83 rebounds and 10.43 assists.

The fifth player is Oscar who came close **five** times: 30.49 points, 9.72 assists and 10.08 rebounds in the 60/61 season; 28.30 points, 9.48 assists and 10.44 rebounds in the 62/63 season; 31.39 points, 10.99 assists and 9.91 rebounds in the 63/64 season; 30.39 points, 8.99 assists and 11.48 rebounds in the 64/65 season; and 31.29 points, 11.14 assists and 7.71 rebounds in the 65/66 season.

He was inducted into Helms Foundation and Naismith Basketball Halls of Fame in 1980 and into the Indiana Basketball Hall of Fame in 1982.

Synopsis of Oscar's Career Accomplishments:

High School

- Two time Indiana State Champion
- Member of 1st undefeated Indiana State Champion
- Mr. Basketball 1956

College

- Led Cincinnati to a 79-9 record (89.77%) during his 3 seasons (1957/58 -1959/60)
- Played in two Final 4's
- Three time consensus All-American
- Three time College Player of the Year (UPI, Sporting News)
- Held NCAA Basketball career scoring record when he left college
- Set 14 NCAA Records
- Won the first two NCAA Division I Player of the Year awards as selected by the United States Basketball Writers Association
- NCAA Player of the Year trophy named the Oscar Robertson award since 1988.
- One of the first five members voted into the National Collegiate Basketball Hall of Fame.
- Olympic gold medalist in 1960

NBA
- 1960/61 NBA Rookie of the Year
- 1963/64 NBA MVP; the only player not named Chamberlain or Russell to win the award in the 60's.
- 1971 NBA Championship
- All NBA 1st Team 9 times
- All NBA 2nd Team twice
- Twelve time NBA All-Star
- Number 14 jersey retired by Sacramento
- Number 1 jersey retired by Milwaukee
- Selected as one of the 50 Greatest Players in NBA History in 1996

Impact on Player Salaries: The Oscar Robertson Suit

Every player today owes a piece of his paycheck to Oscar Robertson.

The Oscar Robertson suit, i.e. *Robertson v. National Basketball Association*, 556 F.2d 682, was the anti-trust suit filed by Oscar as President of and on behalf of the NBA Players Association against the NBA that resulted in the basis for the free agency NBA players benefit from today.

Before Oscar's case, every NBA contract had an "option clause" that basically said, the team had sole rights to the player until the team decided to trade, waive or cut the player. Contract negotiations were simple: accept the team's offer or don't play.

The American Basketball Association was started in 1967 and by 1970 it had become a thorn in the side of NBA owners. They lost stars such a Rick Barry to the upstart league because the ABA was willing to pay a lot more money. Top rookies such as Julius Erving and George McGinnis left school early (not permitted by the NBA) for the "big bucks" in the ABA. This madness had to stop and the leagues began discussing a merger in 1970.

Oscar was President of the NBA Players Union. The players certainly did not want to lose an opportunity to market themselves in a more open market. And Oscar sued the NBA in federal court as an anti-trust case. His argument was that the option clause was a form of trade restraint on the players. He also successfully petitioned to halt the merger of the two leagues from proceeding until the case was resolved.

The negotiations lasted six years until the parties agreed to a resolution. The final agreement seems today to be an obvious and fair compromise – when a contract expires, a player can negotiate with any team he wants with their current team having the right to match the offer to retain the player[11]. This case established the basis of the free agency that benefits players today.

This is why "Every player today owes a piece of his paycheck to Oscar Robertson."

---

[11] Today this form of free agency is called "Restricted Free Agency" (RFA) and applies only to players who have played less than four years or have been released by their teams

Clyde Lovellette

Clyde Lovellette was born September 7, 1929, in Petersburg, Indiana, and graduated from Terre Haute Garfield in 1948. He was one of the first big men (6' 9") to be able to face the basket and play outside as well as inside. His junior year at Garfield he led the team to the state finals where they finished runner-up to Shelbyville and 1947 Mr. Basketball, Bill Garrett. He played college ball at Kansas for Phogg Allen.

At Kansas Clyde became one of the most dominating players in college basketball. One of his teammates was Dean Smith. In his senior year he led the Jayhawks to the 1952 NCAA championship scoring 141 points (the Tournament record at that time) and won the Most Outstanding Player award. He led the nation in scoring at 28.4 points per game becoming, to this day, the only player in NCAA history to lead the nation in scoring and win the NCAA Tournament in the same season. He was named the Helms College Player of the Year. He played just three years because freshmen were not eligible to play varsity and is still KU's fourth-leading scorer with 1,979 points. Kansas honored him by naming their Most Improved Player award the *Clyde Lovellette* award.

His success at Kansas led USOC to select him for the 1952 US Olympics team. He led the team in scoring and to the gold medal in Helsinki.

He was drafted by the Minneapolis Lakers at the tail end of George Mikan's career. He played only 17 minutes per game backing up Mikan his rookie year but became a star in his 2nd year playing 33.7 minutes per game and averaging 18.7 points. His ability to go outside created a mismatch against most of the big men of his time. When they came out to guard him, his quickness enabled him to go right around them. If they didn't come out, he shot over them.

Clyde played in 704 games over 11 seasons for the Lakers, Cincinnati Royals, St. Louis Hawks, and ended his career as Bill Russell's backup for the Celtics where he was an integral part of their 1963 and '64 NBA Championships. He is the only player in NBA history to win championships with both the Lakers and the Celtics.

He was the first person ever to play on NCAA, Olympic, AAU, and NBA championship teams. He was inducted into Indiana Basketball Hall of Fame in 1982 and the Naismith Memorial Basketball Hall of Fame in 1988.

Synopsis of Clyde's Career Accomplishments:

- Indiana High School State Tournament Runner-up, 1947
- Two-time All American: 1951, 1952
- NCAA National Championship, 1952
- Helms Foundation College Player of the Year, 1952
- NCAA Tournament Most Outstanding Player, 1952
- Set NCAA Tournament scoring record with 141 points
- Set NCAA Tournament single game scoring record with 44
- Gold medalist and leading scorer in 1952 Olympics
- AAU Championship, 1953
- Three-time NBA championship: 1954, 1963, and 1964
- Three-time All-NBA second team: 1955, 1956
- Only player in history to win championships with both the Lakers and Celtics

Why Indiana is the Center of the Basketball World

Larry Bird

His story is familiar to everyone. The "Hick from French Lick", born in West Baden Springs, IN, on December 7, 1956; went to IU but was intimidated by the "big city" – Bloomington, Indiana; dropped out and went home to work on a garbage truck. He was talked into enrolling at ISU by another French Lick athlete who had gone to ISU. Larry went on to become one of college basketball's most notable players ever.

For his college career, he averaged 30.3 points, 13.3 rebounds, and 4.6 assists per game, leading the Sycamores to an 81–13 record

Bird-Magic Rivalry

Larry was drafted by the Celtics after his Junior year, but decided to stay at ISU and complete his degree. That decision led to the single greatest factor for the resurrection of the NBA. Who knows what would have happened had he decided to leave early. By coming back he captured the imagination of every basketball fan – avid and casual. After losing their head coach early to health problems, he led ISU to an undefeated regular season and then continued his dominance in the tournament defeating everyone until the finals where they lost to Magic Johnson and Michigan State in what is still the most viewed NCAA game in history.

That was the beginning of a rivalry that grew in the NBA that many feel resurrected professional basketball. With the merger of the NBA and ABA in 1976, professional basketball had become a league of individuals. Many basketball purists felt that the professional game had degenerated to a one-on-one competition that was only interesting in the fourth quarter. The league's rule that zone defenses were illegal made it conducive for stars to take turns going one-on-one against their opposition. Defense was played by a few renegades and the concept of team play was an afterthought.

Impact on the Celtics

Larry's impact on the Celtics was immediate. They went from 29 wins the season before to 61 wins his first year (1979-80) and made to the Eastern Conference Finals for the first time in five years. He followed that up with a 62 win season and the NBA Championship. This despite the fact that a severely broken finger that occurred in a softball game in the summer before his rookie year affected both his field goal shooting (the lowest until his back injury in 1988) and free throw shooting (the lowest of his career).

Celtic attendance increased 43% Larry's first year and remained above 14,000 per game for the duration of his career. The Celtics won 60 games or more 6 times with a high of 67 in the 85-86 season. They won at least 51 games every year Larry played except for the 1988-89 season when Larry played in only 6 games. Boston went to the Finals five times winning three times. They played Magic's Lakers three times winning once.

Impact on the NBA

Larry's impact on the NBA was also immediate. His hardnosed, take no prisoners attitude and his all-around game prompted Dr. J to respond to the question, "What do you think of that rookie, Larry Bird?" with "What rookie!"

Larry and Magic also greatly affected fan interest in the NBA. When they entered the league the NBA Finals were not televised in prime time due to low ratings. They were rebroadcast at 11:30PM and ratings were under 10. Larry's first trip to the Finals was highlighted by Moses

Malone saying on television that he could take four players off the street and beat the Celtics. He was wrong but his comments hurt the ratings. The next year the Finals were broadcast in prime time and ratings doubled. Ratings took another significant jump (from 12.3 to 13.7) in the 1985 rematch between the Lakers and Celtics and continued to be high when the Lakers or the Celtics played in them and then soared again to as high as 18.7 when Michael and the Bulls played in them.

He was inducted into Helms Foundation and Naismith Basketball Hall of Fame in 1998 and into the Indiana Basketball Hall of fame in 2000.

Impact on Player Salaries: The Larry Bird Exceptions

Every player today owes a piece of his paycheck to Larry Bird.

Nowhere is the impact of Larry Bird felt more than in salaries NBA players earn today. When Larry joined the league the players' average salary was $189,000. When he retired the *average* salary was $1,034,000.

However, free agency had a negative impact on one of the NBA's strongest selling points: player loyalty. Fans followed their home team heroes and felt personal relationship with them through their town. Players' ability to leave for more money tainted that loyalty and, consequently, their following.

Also, teams that spent the most got the best players. This may have helped with TV ratings and "super teams" attendance. But it hurt the attendance of teams that could not afford big name players. It also reduced local following which reduced local TV revenues.

The league implemented salary caps in 1984-85 season to "level the playing field" and increase competition. However, this did not address the problem of stars leaving their teams and cities to move to a team that had more cap room. They realized that stars, such as Larry Bird, leaving their team could severely hurt the league. They wanted to maintain the rivalries and traditions that were playing so well with their increased audience.

Therefore, they implemented the "Larry Bird Exception" whereby teams could re-sign their own players for more years (6) and bigger annual raises than if they signed with another team even if they exceeded the cap.

This was followed by another exception called the "Early Bird Exception" that allows teams to re-sign their free agents with a first-year salary up to the average league salary or 175 percent of the player's previous salary, whichever is higher, and contracts for five or less years.

The final exception to signing players to contracts that exceed the cap is the "Non-Bird Exception" whereby a team can re-sign its free agents for 120 percent of the minimum salary, whatever the amount of a qualifying offer if the player is a restricted free agent, or 120 percent of the player's previous salary for five or less years.

These "Bird" exceptions and the continued popularity of basketball have led to huge contracts and an **average** salary in 2017 of $6,676,762.

The "Bird Exceptions" may not have taken the cap off of salaries; but at least it made the NBA doff it.

That is why "Every player today owes a piece of his paycheck to Larry Bird".

Synopsis of Larry's Career Accomplishments:

College
- Third Team All-American: 1977
- Two-time first team All American: 1978 & 1979
- Won all eight NCAA player-of-the-year awards in 1979
- Undefeated regular season 1978-79
- NCAA Runner-up 1979

NBA
- NBA Rookie of the Year in 1980
- Three-time NBA MVP: 1984-1986
- Three-time NBA championship: 1981, 1984, and 1986
- Two-time Finals MVP: 1984, 1986
- Olympic gold medalist in 1992 with the original "Dream Team"
- Twelve-time NBA All-Star
- Nine-time All-NBA first team: 1980-1988
- Three-time All NBA Defensive 2nd Team: 1981-1983
- One of the 50 Greatest Players in NBA History: 1996
- Three-time winner of NBA long distance shooting contest: 1986-1988
- Named NBA Coach of the Year in 1998
- Named Executive of the year in 2011 becoming the first person in the history of the NBA to be named Player of the year, Coach of the Year, and Executive of the Year

Synopsis of Larry's Unreal Accomplishments

Larry was the eight-time winner of the MITT (Most Irritating Trash Talker) Award. He was notorious for his colorful "banter" and the irritating way he was always able to back it up. He would tell the man guarding him what he was going to do; and then do it!

One of his most famous trash talking exploits was at the first three-point shooting contest in 1986. He walked into the locker room where the contestants were getting ready and asked, "Which one of you guys is gonna' get second?" He then, of course, went out and won it not only that year, but again in the next two years before graciously bowing out of the competition to let someone else have a chance.

He was voted by his peers into the TT-HOF (Trash Talking Hall of Fame) immediately upon his retirement. At his non-induction one player said, "Thank God that [SOB] has retired. Maybe my nightmares of guarding him will finally stop."

Louie Dampier

Probably the least pretentious person in the Hall of Fame,[12] Louie Dampier was born in Indianapolis on November 20, 1944. A graduate of Southport High School (1963), he played for Adolph Rupp at Kentucky and with fellow Hoosier Tommy Kron and Pat Riley (his roommate for four years) led "Rupp's Runts" to one of the most historic NCAA Tournament final games - their 1966 upset by the first all-black team, Texas Western, now named UTEP (University of Texas at El Paso). While at Kentucky he was All-SEC three times, All-American twice and an Academic All-American. When he graduated he was Kentucky's third all-time leading scorer (1575 points in three seasons).

He was drafted by the Cincinnati Royals but eschewed the opportunity to play with Oscar and accepted a contract with the Kentucky Colonels of the newly formed ABA. He played for them all nine of their ABA seasons and is the ABA career leader in games played (728), minutes played (27,770), points scored (13,726), and assists (4,044). His 794 three point field goals are 288 more than fellow Hoosier Billy Keller's second most. His 35.8% career three point percent is fifth best. A career 82.0% free throw shooter, he made fifty-seven consecutively in the 1970-71 season.

When the ABA folded, Louie was drafted by the San Antonio Spurs and hit 48.8% of his field goal attempts backing up George Gervin. In 1999 the newly formed ABA Semi-Pro League named one of their divisions the Louis Dampier Division.

He was inducted into the Indiana Basketball Hall of Fame in 1993 and into the Naismith Hall of Fame in 2015. He has his Southport High School jersey hung for his Hall of Fame exhibit.

Synopsis of Louie's Career Accomplishments:

- Two time Consensus second-team All-American (1966, 1967)
- Three time All-SEC
- ABA champion (1975)
- Seven time ABA All-Star (1968–1970, 1972–1975)
- Four time All-ABA Second Team (1968–1970, 1974)
- ABA All-Rookie First Team (1968)
- ABA All-Time Team

[12] An excellent example of this is his opening story in his Hall Of Fame acceptance speech
http://www.nba.com/video/channels/hall_of_fame/2015/09/12/20150911-hof-speech-dampier.nba

George McGinnis

George McGinnis was born on August 12, 1950, in Indianapolis. He went to Indianapolis Washington High School where he was an All American in two sports – basketball and football. His size, 6'8", 235 pounds, was imposing enough. What made him awesome was the fact that he was also extremely quick and agile. He played end on the football team and defensive backs could not tackle him one-on-one.

But basketball was his first love. He led the Continentals his senior year to an undefeated season and state championship (1969), only the third team in Indiana history to finish undefeated. He set scoring records for the four Sweet Sixteen games (148) including 49 against Jac-Cen-Del in the semi-state. He is the only person who is in the top ten scoring for the final two games (8th with 62 points) and the top five in rebounding for the final two games (3rd with 41 rebounds). His 27 rebounds in the final game was a record at that time and is the second most today.

He was the consensus Mr. Basketball and led the Indiana All-Stars to a 91-83 win in the first game at Hinkle Field House against the Kentucky All-Stars with 23 points and 14 rebounds. Kentucky All-Star Joe Voskuhl, father of Jake Voshkuhl - UConn's 2000 NCAA Championship starting center and 9 year NBA veteran, was quoted as saying he thought George was overrated. Big George went to Louisville with something to prove. And he certainly did. In one of the greatest exhibits of basketball at any level, George ripped Kentucky for 53 points and 31 rebounds as Indiana trounced Kentucky 114-83.

George went to IU when freshmen were not allowed by NCAA rules to play varsity. He and Washington teammate, 6' 9" Steve Downing, led the freshmen to a convincing win in the annual Freshman-Varsity basketball game whetting the appetite of IU fans everywhere. He did not disappoint. He led the Hoosiers and the Big Ten in scoring (29.9) and rebounding (14.7) his sophomore year, only the fifth player and the first sophomore in Big Ten history to do so. He scored 30 or more points 13 times with a single game high of 45. Dave Winfield, starting forward at Minnesota that year, credits George with helping him decide on a professional career in baseball rather than basketball.

Bob Knight replaced Lou Watson in what would have been George's Junior year. But the death of George's father weeks after his phenomenal performance in the Indiana-Kentucky All-Star game and the lure of the money his hometown Pacers offered ($30,000 signing bonus and $250,000 per year) incented George to jump into the ranks of professional basketball.

His four years in the ABA were the most productive of his professional career. He helped the fledgling league gain credibility and became one of its most productive players. He was all ABA first team twice and second team once. He led the league in scoring in the 1974-75 season. He helped the Pacers win two ABA Championships (1972 & 1973) and was outstanding in the 1975 playoffs scoring 32.3 points, grabbing 15.9 rebounds and dishing out 8.2 assists per game carrying the Pacers to the finals.

In 1975 George jumped to the NBA and signed with the New York Knicks. Philadelphia, who had drafted George in 1973, intervened saying they had the rights to George. They signed him to a six year $3 million contract and began George's NBA career. The 76ers had won only 34 games in the 1974-75 season which, as bad as it was, was the total number of wins of the preceding two seasons. Basketball was dying in a city that had been a playoff team for 21 consecutive years until 1972. They really needed something to re-instill the fan base. And General Manager Pat Williams thought George was the answer. Again, he didn't disappoint.

George averaged 23 points and 12.6 rebounds his first season as the 76ers won 46 games and made the playoffs for the first time since 1970-71. Attendance increased by more than 71%, from just under 5,200 per game to 12,431 per game and more than 500,000 annually for the first time in Philadelphia history[13]. Coach Gene Shue said, "I don't know how many games that first year he just took over and won by doing something great on his own."[14] They made the playoffs and the phrase "Let George do it" became the most popular slogan in Philadelphia. He averaged 29.8 points, 14.3 rebounds and 6.3 assists per game. He gave instant credibility to the quality of play of the ABA and provided greater incentive for the NBA to conclude their merger talks.

The following year Philadelphia signed another ABA superstar – Julius Erving. George's stats declined slightly to 23.0 points per game, 12.6 rebounds and 4.7 assists. But the addition of Dr. J's 21.6 points, 8.5 rebounds and 3.7 assists enabled the 76ers to reach the NBA Finals where they lost an epic battle to the Bill Walton led Portland Trailblazers.

He played one more year in Philadelphia averaging a third straight 20+ points and 10+ rebounds making it to the Conference Finals. He was traded to Denver in 1978 and averaged a fourth straight double-double, 22.6 points and 11.4 rebounds. He was traded back to the Pacers in the middle of the '79-80 season and finished his career there.

He was inducted into the Indiana Basketball Hall of Fame in 1995 and into the Naismith Hall of Fame in 2017.

Synopsis of George's Career Accomplishments:

High School
- 1969 Indiana High School Basketball Championship
- 1969 Mr. Basketball
- Scored 53 points and grabbed 31 rebounds in Indiana-Kentucky All-Star game

College
- All-American Third Team (1971)
- Named to IU's All-Century Team, 2000

ABA
- ABA championship: 1972, 1973
- Second Team All-ABA (1973)
- Three time ABA All-Star (1973–1975)
- Three time All-ABA First Team (1974–1976)
- ABA Co-MVP (1975)
- Won the ABA scoring title in 1975
- Number retired by Indiana Pacers
- Member of the ABA's All-Time Team

NBA
- First Team All-NBA selection in 1976
- Second Team All-NBA selection in 1977
- Three NBA All-Star selections (1976, 1977, 1979)

---

[13] http://www.rodneyfort.com/PHSportsEcon/Common/OtherData/NBAAttendance/NBAAttendance.html
[14] http://sportsillustrated.cnn.com/vault/article/magazine/MAG1125273/2/index.htm

Coaches

This study measured each state's concentration of coaches in the NBA, NCAA Division I, and Naismith Hall of Fame.

NBA

There have been 323 persons who have been head coach in at least one game in the NBA. Seventeen states have only provided one coach; seven states only two; only sixteen have provided five or more and 80.7% (263) of coaches in NBA history come from these sixteen states.

Twenty-nine coaches (9.4%) have come from Indiana. Twelve coached less than one year (82 GC). Five coached less than 10 total regular season games. Ninety-one coaches (30.4%) have career regular season winning percentages of at least 50%. Nine of these are from Indiana (31.0% of the Indiana coaches).

Table SO-5 displays the concentrations for ranges of games coached (GC). In the history of the NBA **Indiana's 5.632/million is the highest Concentration of coaches,** 2.5 more than New York's 2nd highest concentration and more than twice New Jersey's 3rd highest.

Indiana has the highest concentration for all ranges up to 899 GC surpassed by .087 by Utah's one coach (Dick Motta) for these ranges.

Only 94 coaches have coached 400+ games. Seventy-six of these (80.9%) come from the ten states that produced 3+ coaches. Twelve states have produced the only twenty-nine coaches with 1000+ GC. Indiana is one of four states to have produced 3 or more.

NCAA Division I

There have been 1725 persons who have been head coach for at least 100 NCAA Division I games since 1895. One hundred and seven (107) of these (6.2%) have come from Indiana. Table SO-6 shows the Concentration of coaches for each State. **Indiana's 107 coaches computes to a Concentration of 26.455 per million, 5.334 persons per million more than the second highest,** Utah's 21.121 per million.

SO-6 displays concentrations for time periods 1895-1929, 1930-1949, each decade from the 50's through the 90's and since 2000. It shows that **Indiana is the most consistent producer of NCAA coaches** with no less than the 4th highest concentration for seven of the nine time periods (10th in the 50's and 8th in the 70's), and is the only state to provide coaches with no less than the 10th highest concentration for every time period, and the highest concentration this century.

Table SO-7 displays the concentration of coaches from each state for ranges of minimum games coached. Indiana is the only state to provide coaches with no less than the 10th highest concentration for any range of games coached.

Kansas has the most impressive results with the highest concentration for every range from 800+ and no lower than the 5th highest concentration for every range starting with 400 or more games coached.

Only twenty-nine (29) coaches have coached 1000+ games. Kansas has produced the most with Lon Kruger and Hall of Famers Dean Smith, Adolph Rupp, and Frank Miller. Indiana's lone 1000+ games coached is Steve Alford.

Current coaches near the 1000 games coached include Jim Laranaga (Miami-FL) 989; John Calipari (Kentucky) 955; Dana Altman (Oregon) 936; Leonard Hamilton (Florida State) 925; and Tubby Smith (Memphis) 909.

Hall of Fame

There are 103 persons inducted into the Naismith Memorial Hall of Fame as coaches. Table SO-HOF shows that Indiana's six Hall of Fame coaches yields the 3rd largest concentration (1.165) less than half the concentration the six coaches from Kansas yields and .049 less than Mississippi's three coaches computed concentration.

John Wooden

Wooden began his coaching career at Dayton High School in Kentucky across the river from Cincinnati while playing for the Kautsky's in Indianapolis. He finished 6-11, the only losing season he would ever have. He followed that season with a 15-3 record and an opportunity to return to Indiana and coach South Bend Central.

He coached South Bend Central for nine seasons winning three Sectionals and two Regionals while compiling an impressive record of 197-28 (88%) despite having to practice at the local YMCA due to the school's poor facilities. His tenure at SB Central was interrupted by World War II and upon his return in 1947 he started the most successful college coaching career by anyone at Indiana State Teacher's College, now Indiana State University.

Wooden led the Sycamores to an impressive 17-8 record his first year and an invitation to the NAIB (National Association of Intercollegiate Basketball) national playoffs. Wooden's character and respect for all men prohibited him from accepting the invitation. The NAIB prohibited black players from participating and Wooden, despite being raised in a stronghold of the Ku Klux Klan (Martinsville in the 20's), would not support such an injustice because he had one black player on the team even though that one player was a reserve.

The following year, State finished 27-7 and the NAIB, now allowing black players to participate, again invited Wooden's team to the tournament. He again declined the invitation because, though they were allowed to play, blacks were not allowed to be photographed or seen in public with the rest of the team. He changed his position at the urging of the NAACP and with the approval of the player's, Clarence Walker's, parents. They got to the final game where they were defeated by Louisville.

His 44-15 (75%) record and runner-up in the NAIB propelled Wooden into the national limelight and major schools came calling. His beloved alma mater wanted him to become an assistant and take over when coach, Mel Taube, retired. Wooden refused thinking that move would undermine Taube's authority.

Among the schools courting Wooden were Minnesota and UCLA. Wooden was really hoping that Minnesota would make him an offer as he really wanted to coach in the Big Ten. However, when the time they said they would call if interested came and passed, he thought they were not interested and accepted UCLA's offer. What he did not know was that weather in Minnesota had made telephoning impossible at the designated time. When they finally were able to get through later that night, Wooden informed them that, as sorry as he was, he could not accept the position because he had already accepted UCLA's offer. This would not be Minnesota's only failed attempt to get a hall of fame coach with Indiana ties who wanted to coach there.

Wooden came to a UCLA team that had had limited or no success and played in a gym that sat 3000 *fewer* fans than his Martinsville High School gym. He turned the program around immediately going 22-7 his first year and 24-7 in his second. Meanwhile, Mel Taube had retired at Purdue and they came calling with a far more lucrative offer than what he was making at UCLA. Finally, his dream job within his grasp, he asked UCLA to let him out of the third year of his contract. They declined reminding him that it was he who demanded a three year deal. He informed Purdue that he would not be able come until the next year, hoping they would wait. They did not and the rest is, literally, history.

Who knows what would have happened had Purdue had the wisdom to wait a year. Would the "Wizard of Westwood" have become the "Legend of Lafayette?"[15] I grew up hearing this story from my mother who was raised six blocks from Ross Ade Stadium and whose father worked for Purdue for 47 years. She told me that she never saw her father madder in his life than when Purdue decided not to wait for Wooden. How could they know they would be losing the opportunity to have "the greatest coach of all time in any sport"?[16]

His coaching accomplishments at UCLA are historic. His tournament winning percentage of 88.46% is fourth highest. The three persons with higher tournament winning percentages have a total of six combined number of appearances in the tournament, ten less than Wooden: Ed Jucker who only lost one game in the three tournaments he coached Cincinnati, the 1963 Final Game; Ken Loeffler (LaSalle) who won one NCAA Tournament and finished as Runner-up in his other appearance; and fellow Hoosier Everett Dean who only coached in one tournament while at Stanford and won it for the only perfect 100% winning percentage in history.

His records for consecutive championships (7), consecutive tournament wins (38), consecutive regular season wins (88), consecutive home court wins (98), appearances in the Final Four (16), consecutive Final Four appearances (9), and total Final Four victories (21) will probably never be approached let alone surpassed. He won 80.83% of the 620 games he coached at UCLA, 82.5% of his Pac-10 games and 80.39% of all of the college games he coached. Of all of the coaches who have at least ten years NCAA coaching only Adolph Rupp's 82.18% winning percentage bests Wooden's.

My response to critics who say he was only able to win so many games and championships because of the quality of the talent he was able to recruit is that they do not really understand basketball and the issues in developing a winning *team*. Wooden understood it. When asked by Rick Reilly how many championships he thought Kobe Bryant could win his reply was, "None. Kobe doesn't win championships. The Lakers win championships."[17]

But all of his basketball accomplishments pale in comparison to his contributions to humanity. His Pyramid of Success is a blueprint for righteous living. Begun in 1934 and finished in 1948, it is a summation of all that he learned from his parents, teachers, coaches, his wife Nellie and his life experiences.

One of the greatest lessons I learned from Coach Wooden is the difference between commanding respect versus *demanding* respect. There are too many people who, because of their occupation or position or wealth or looks or whatever, demand respect from anyone and everyone. They often treat others as underlings or disrespect them. Too many sports figures and movie stars today have this affliction and it often gets them in trouble.

---

[15] With apologies to my late mother and all other West Lafayette residents, I know Purdue is in West Lafayette. But the "Legend of West Lafayette" loses the alliterative allure that nicknames are so fond of having.

[16] As selected in 2009 by a panel of more than 100 past and present coaches convened by Sporting News.

[17] "Wooden Set the Bar High" by Rick Reilly, http://sports.espn.go.com/espn/news/story?id=5260677

Why Indiana is the Center of the Basketball World

With all of the accolades Coach Wooden was showered with, he could easily have had a superior attitude. But he never did. He treated all persons with respect, even those he did not particularly care for. He would respect these persons from afar. It is why all of his players respected and loved him. He respected their individuality even if he did not necessarily agree with it.

It is why he could understand and coach so many distinct personalities and get them to play together as a team. He instilled basic moralities without trying to direct the paths of their lives. He coached Bill Walton, the hippie, and Lew Alcindor, the intense African-American from New York City who was an advocate of black pride and later changed his name to Kareem Abdul-Jabbar to name just two of the many personalities who played for and respected Coach Wooden.

"To lead the way Coach Wooden led takes a tremendous amount of faith. He was almost mystical in his approach, yet that approach only strengthened our confidence. Coach Wooden enjoyed winning, but he did not put winning above everything. He was more concerned that we became successful as human beings, that we earned our degrees, that we learned to make the right choices as adults and as parents. In essence," Abdul-Jabbar concluded, "he was preparing us for life."[18]

Bill Walton summed him up when he said, "He didn't teach basketball. He taught life."[19]

The underlying core of Coach Wooden's being was his righteousness and piety. He said "Material possessions, winning scores, and great reputations are meaningless in the eyes of the Lord, because He knows what we really are and that is all that matters." And he lived that way. He never made more than $35,000 in salary even though he was offered millions to coach the Lakers and others.

He valued truth, honesty, friendship and basketball. But, the most valuable thing in his life was his wife Nellie. Even after she died she was always with him in his head, in his heart, and in his soul.

He was inducted to the Naismith Hall of Fame as a coach in 1973, the first person inducted as a player and a coach.

Awards won:

1960: **Inducted into the Naismith Basketball Hall of Fame as a player** with fellow Hoosiers Branch McCracken and Stretch Murphy, the first Hoosier natives so honored

1962: **Inducted into the Indiana Basketball Hall of Fame**

1964, 1967, 1969, 1970, 1972, 1973: **NCAA Coach of the Year**

1973: **Inducted into the Naismith Basketball Hall of Fame as a coach** the first person to be inducted as both a player and a coach

1977: **The John R. Wooden Award** given to college basketball's premier player-of-the-year is named in his honor

1995: The **Theodore Roosevelt Award**, the NCAA's highest honor.

---

[18] John Wooden, Who Built Incomparable Dynasty at U.C.L.A., Dies at 99, FRANK LITSKY and JOHN BRANCH, NY Times, June 4, 2010, and published online at
http://www.nytimes.com/2010/06/05/sports/ncaabasketball/05wooden.html?pagewanted=3&_r=1
[19] *Legend lost: Former UCLA coach John Wooden, 99, dies,* David Leon Moore, USA TODAY, June 14, 2010,
http://www.usatoday.com/sports/college/mensbasketball/2010-06-04-john-wooden-obit_N.htm

Why Indiana is the Center of the Basketball World

2000: The **John R. Wooden Tradition**, a four-team early season college basketball showcase.

2003: The **Presidential Medal of Freedom**, America's highest civilian honor.

2005: The **Sachem**, Indiana's highest honor, for a lifetime of excellence and moral virtue that has brought credit and honor to Indiana.

2006: The **Gerald R. Ford Award** for advocacy for intercollegiate sports throughout a career.

2006: Member of the founding class of the **National Collegiate Basketball Hall of Fame** with Dr. James Naismith, Oscar Robertson, Bill Russell and Dean Smith.

2009: Selected as **"The Greatest Coach of All Time"** in any sport by a panel of more than 100 past and present coaches convened by Sporting News.

Paul D. "Tony" Hinkle

John Wooden once called Tony Hinkle, "The greatest coach that ever lived."[20] He was born in 1898 in Logansport, Indiana, IN. He graduated in 1917 from Calumet High School in the Region and attended the University of Chicago when it was in the Big Ten graduating in 1921. He lettered three years in basketball. As captain of the 1919/20 team, he led them to the Big Ten championship losing the national championship (as selected by the Helm's Committee) to Penn and was selected as a Helm's All-American that year.

He also played football at Chicago for legendary coach Alonzo Stagg and was a star on the baseball team as well. It is a tribute to his skill as a footballer that when Stagg told Hinkle to quit baseball to attend spring football practices or be kicked off the team, Hinkle declined and Stagg relented. He was a great baseball player as well and was asked by John McGraw to join the New York Giants. However, Hinkle whose specialty was the spitball, which had been outlawed the year before, decided his future was in coaching. It was also at Chicago that he was nicknamed "Tony" by his baseball coach.

Stagg had assumed the head basketball coaching position at Chicago when Pat Page resigned and went to Butler. He asked Hinkle to serve as an assistant. However, Page asked Hinkle to join him at Butler and Tony, questioning Stagg's desire to really have him there, accepted and moved to Indianapolis in 1921 to begin a half century of service to Butler and the Indianapolis community. He served as football and baseball coach as well as basketball coach and won more than 1000 combined games in these sports.

He became head basketball coach in the 26/27 season and retained that position through the 69/70 season taking off three years (42/43 through 44/45) to serve in World War II. His teams won 560 games while losing only 392 (58.8%) including a national championship in 1929. He always scheduled as many major conference schools as would play him and his success against these schools gained Butler the reputation as the "giant killer."

The Hinkle System

Tony developed an offense that involved all five players and created shot opportunities for everyone using constant ball and player movement, pick and roll fundamentals, and weak side picks. Hinkle developed drills for every situation that taught each player their positioning in each situation and the variations that were determined by the way the defense played it. It was an early "motion offense" that encouraged every player to shoot when they got open to take "their shot." It is a system that enabled fourteen of his players to become Indiana Hall of Fame high school coaches including my high school coach, Bill Shepherd. It enabled the offensively gifted to succeed as evidenced by the success of Billy and Dave Shepherd at Carmel.

Hinkle Field House

When it was built in 1928, the Butler Field House was the largest basketball arena in the country and remained so for decades. It housed the finals of the Indiana State High School Basketball Tournament until 1971. It is where the movie *Hoosiers* filmed its dramatic final game and is still a historic landmark. It was appropriately renamed the Tony Hinkle Memorial Field House in 1966.

---

[20] http://sports.espn.go.com/travel/news/story?id=4748977

Tony Hinkle's Butler Coaching Record all sports:

	Years	Won	Lost	Tied	Pct.
Football	1926, '35-'41, '46-'69	165	99	13	.619
Basketball	1926-'42, '45-'70	560	392	0	.588
Baseball	1921-'28, '33-'41, '46-'70	335	309	5	.520
Totals		1060	800	18	.569

Tony was inducted into the Indiana Basketball Hall of Fame in 1964 and enshrined in the Naismith Basketball Hall of Fame as a Contributor in 1965.

"Piggy" Lambert

Ward "Piggy" Lambert was born in 1888 in Deadwood, South Dakota. His family relocated to Crawfordsville in 1890 and he graduated from Crawfordsville High School in 1908. Although he never played basketball in high school, he played basketball, football and baseball at Wabash despite weighing only 114 pounds. He graduated in 1911. He got the nickname "Piggy" for his reluctance to give up the ball once he had it.

He began his coaching career at Lebanon High School in 1912. He went to Purdue for the 1916/17 season and then went into the service for World War I returning to Purdue for the 1918/19 season where coached through the 1945/46 season. He won 371 of the 523 games he coached (70.9%) and 228 of his 333 conference games (68.4%). His 1932 team was selected by the Helm's Foundation as the national champions. It included future Hall of Famers Stretch Murphy and John Wooden who credited Lambert as one of the people whose principles formed his Pyramid of Success. He is tied with Bob Knight for the most Big Ten basketball titles with eleven and is third behind Knight and Gene Keady in total wins and conference wins while a Big Ten coach. He coached sixteen All Americans and 31 first team All-Big Ten players. He was selected as the nation's best coach by *Esquire* magazine in 1945.

Fast Break Pioneer

His greatest contribution to the game was his pioneering of the fast-break style of play.[21] He always recruited big men who had quickness and could handle the ball and guards who could play ball hawking defense and transition basketball. In 1932 he wrote one the first textbooks on basketball, *Practical Basketball,* which influenced coaches for years.

Lambert Fieldhouse (originally known as Purdue Fieldhouse), Purdue's basketball arena before Mackey Arena, was named in his honor. It is currently used as the indoor track and field facility. Lambert also coached Purdue's baseball team in 1917, from 1919 to 1935 and from 1945 to 1946. Lambert Field, Purdue's former baseball stadium, is also named for Piggy.

After retiring from Purdue, he became Commissioner of the National Basketball League during the final three years (1946–49) of their existence. He was one of the key people that drove the NBL's merger the Basketball Association of America, their offspring becoming the National Basketball Association.

He was inducted into the Naismith Memorial Basketball Hall of Fame and the Helms Foundation Hall of Fame in 1960 and the Indiana Basketball Hall of Fame in 1962.

---

[21] http://www.hoophall.com/hall-of-famers/tag/ward-l-lambert

Everett S. Dean "The Gentleman from Indiana"

Everett Dean was born in Livonia, IN, March 18, 1898, and graduated from Salem High School in 1917. From there he went to IU where he played for three years gaining a Helm's All-American award in 1921. He began his coaching career at small Carleton College and returned to IU in 1924 to become their head coach.

He coached IU for fourteen years compiling a 162-93 overall record (63.5%) and a 96-72 Big Ten Conference record (57.1%). He had only three losing seasons at IU and won IU's first conference championship in 1926. He shared two more conference championships, 1928 and 1936.

He left Indiana in 1938 to take over the Stanford University basketball program. He coached 11 seasons from the 1938/39 season through the 1950/51 season and compiled a 167-118 overall record (58.6%) and a 68-73 Conference record (48.2%). He has a career record of 375 – 215 (63.3%) twenty-one winning seasons during his twenty-eight seasons.

He is the only undefeated coach in NCAA Tournament history winning the 1942 NCAA Championship the only time his team made the NCAA Tournament. He is the only man to win an NCAA Basketball Championship and an NCAA World Series baseball game (1953).

Known as "the Gentleman from Indiana," Dean wrote two popular basketball books, *Indiana Basketball* (1933) and *Progressive Basketball* (1949) in which he expounded on the benefits of the fast break style of play.

He was enshrined in the Indiana Basketball Hall of Fame in 1965, the Naismith Basketball Hall of Fame in 1966, and is the only person in the Naismith Hall of Fame who is also a member of the College Baseball Hall of Fame.

Slick Leonard

There is no one who more personifies Indiana basketball than Robert, Bobby, "Slick" Leonard, born July 7, 1932, in Terre Haute. Growing up indigent during the Depression, he discovered his calling on a basketball court in a neighbor's backyard. An Indiana All-Star from Terre Haute Gerstmeyer in 1950, he went to IU where he became a two-time All-American and as captain of the 1953 team, fulfilled every players dream: making the game winning free throws to win an NCAA Championship.

He had a solid seven year NBA career (56/57 through 62/63) averaging 27 minutes and 9.9 points per game playing for the Minneapolis/Los Angeles Lakers, Chicago Packers and Chicago Zephyrs. His best year was the 1961/62 season with the Packers when he averaged 35 minutes and 16 points per game.

He got his nickname from teammate George Mikan, who losing at cards to Bobby and asked, "How about buying me a cup of coffee? You're too slick for me."[22] His teammates heard it and agreed with raucous laughter and the name stuck.

He began his coaching career as player/coach for the Chicago Zephyrs in the 1962/63 season and remained the coach for the 63/64 season following the team's moved to Baltimore. In 1968 the Indiana Pacers started the season 2-7 and called on Bobby to replace Larry Staverman and try to resurrect the season. He guided that team all the way to the ABA Finals. In his eight years as coach, the Pacers won 58.9% of their games, made the playoffs every year, made the Finals five times, and won three Championships. He was selected as the All Time ABA Coach in 1997.[23]

He continued as coach for the first four years of the NBA Pacers. With a depleted roster and no first round draft picks until his 3rd year, he won only 41.3%.

Today he is the radio analyst and color commentator for the Pacers. His intelligent insights and entertaining stories delivered in his Indiana drawl have entertained Pacer fans for 29 years. His iconic "**BOOM, BABY**" lets every listener know a Pacer just hit a three pointer.

Indiana high school All-Star; IU All-American; making free throws to win the 1953 NCAA Championship; seven years playing in the NBA; twelve years coaching the Indiana Pacers; 29 years as Pacer radio and TV analyst/commentator; the first person inducted into the Indiana University Sports Hall of Fame; one of only six individuals in Pacers history to have a banner raised in his honor; inducted into the Indiana Basketball Hall of Fame in 1982; and into the Naismith Memorial Basketball Hall of Fame in 2014.

Slick Leonard is the epitome of Indiana basketball.

---

[22] http://www.indystar.com/story/sports/nba/pacers/2014/08/06/bobby-slick-leonard-indiana-pacers-nba-aba/13705925/
[23] https://en.wikipedia.org/wiki/ABA_All-Time_Team#Coaches

Gregg Popovich

Although not currently enshrined in the Naismith Basketball Hall of Fame, there is little doubt that Gregg, "Pop" Popovich will be.

Popovich was born January 28, 1949, in East Chicago, IN. He graduated from Merrillville High School in 1966. He attended the Air Force Academy where he led the team in scoring as captain his senior year. While serving his mandatory five year service, he played on the Armed Forces AAU team and captained the 1972 team that won the AAU Championship. He then served as assistant coach at Air Force for six years earning a Master's degree in physical education from the University of Denver. In 1979 he became head basketball coach at Pomona-Pitzger.

During his time at Pomona he met and became friends with Larry Brown. He even took a one year sabbatical and was a volunteer assistant under Brown for the 1985-86 season at Kansas and was the best man at Larry's 1990 wedding. He joined Brown as lead assistant at San Antonio from 1988 to 1992 when he went to Golden State under Don Nelson.

He returned to San Antonio in 1994 as General Manager and VP of Basketball Operations. After a dismal start to the 1996-97 season (3-16), Popovich assumed the head coaching duties and led the team to the only losing season he has had at San Antonio. In his 20 seasons as head coach since that first year, he has made the playoffs every year. He has coached 1656 games winning 1150 (69.4%) and is 166-106 in the playoffs (61.0%). He's made the Conference Finals ten times, the NBA Finals six times, and has won five NBA Championships. He was voted NBA Coach of the Year in 2003, 2012, and 2014.

He was inducted into the Indiana Basketball Hall of Fame in 2009 and will be enshrined in the Naismith Memorial Hall of Fame soon.

Innovators/Contributors

Innovations are improvements to the way the game is played, coached, officiated, enjoyed by fans, or administered as a sport. There are many people responsible for making changes to the way the game is played.

The primary statistical evidence for this category is the make-up of the Naismith Hall of Fame Contributors.[24] The fifty-eight persons enshrined as Contributors have made innovations to the rules, the game itself, the promotion of the game, etc. Table SO-HOF shows that of the states that have at least 2 million in population, Indiana has the second highest concentration of HOF Contributors behind only Kansas.

This following are descriptions of the Hoosiers who have made significant innovations and their impact on the game and sport of Basketball.

Piggy Lambert (HOF Coach):

Fast-break Pioneer

"Lambert [Ward, Piggy] pioneered the fast-breaking style of hardwood play"[25]

The most significant change to the way the game is played, coached, and enjoyed by fans was the development of fast-break basketball. This is defined as pressure defense, forcing turnovers, and an attacking offense that forces defensive mistakes or odd man situations that create easy shots. It completely changed the way the game was played. Before Lambert basketball was a completely ball control style of offense. Bring it up; get in position; throw the ball around until someone gets an open shot.

Developed by Lambert, adopted early by McCracken and mastered by Wooden, it is the style that best highlights the speed, agility, and jumping required of basketball and is still the most exciting to most fans. They appreciate half-court, ball control offenses executed well. But it's fast-break, show time, up and down, and alley-oops that brings them out of their seats, gets the loudest cheering and creates the most lasting memories.

Its impact on coaching was also monumental. They had to learn it to defend it. They had to understand the type of personnel required to be successful with it. And they had to learn how to implement it, i.e., drills, sets, plays, variations, etc. It was the origin of double teaming, pressing, and motion offenses.

Chuck Taylor (HOF Contributor)

Charles "Chuck" Taylor was born and raised near Columbus, Indiana, on June 24, 1901. He loved basketball and wanted to play it his whole life dreaming of hitting the big shot and becoming a basketball celebrity. He starred at Columbus High School where he was a two-time All-State selection. He turned pro immediately after high school and is said to have played for eleven years for teams in Ft. Wayne, Detroit, Buffalo, Akron and with the original Celtics. This, like many of the stories of the man, is partially true.

---

[24] A person is eligible for Enshrinement as a contributor at any time for significant contributions to the game of basketball. What constitutes a "significant contribution" shall be determined by the BHOF, its Screening Committee(s) or Honors Committee(s). http://www.hoophall.com/enshrinement-process/

[25] http://www.hoophall.com/hall-of-famers/tag/ward-l-lambert

That he wore Converse All Stars when he played is undeniable. That he went to Chicago looking for a job with Converse is also undeniable. And no matter how it really happened, there is absolutely no doubt that he went to work for Converse in 1922 where he found his calling and became the most recognized name in basketball.

Basketball Shoe

Everyone has heard of the Chuck Taylor All Star basketball shoe made by Converse (now owned by Nike). Long before "Air Jordans" hit the scene, the high top, canvas shoe with the familiar logo has been a part of Americana for decades. The official shoe of the Olympics from 1936 to 1968, "Chucks" were *the* shoe not only for basketball, but also for "cool." My daughter, during her Goth period, would only wear black "Chuck Taylors." She, like many people, had no idea that Chuck Taylor was a real person and a member of the Naismith Basketball Hall of Fame.

Converse had been making basketball shoes since 1917. Changes recommended by Taylor were incorporated including adding an ankle patch for protection. That patch became the most recognized symbol in basketball shoes and may be still so today: the Converse All-Star logo. In 1932 "Chuck Taylor" was added to the logo and a star was born.

With no sales experience he went on one of his first sales calls to Knute Rockne at Notre Dame. Rockne told him to look his prospects in the eye and be himself. Thus began a lifelong career as a consummate salesman. He would drive around his sales territory meeting as many people he could talking up basketball and the incredible shoe made by Converse.

He was on the road 365 days of the year living out of his car and in hotels. He did not have a permanent address until later in life and after retirement. Even then he would be on the road most of the year taking his wife with him. He did not have his first permanent residency until he bought a house in California in 1950.

The Basketball Clinic

His playing time with professional or semi-professional basketball teams gave him instant credibility with high school and college coaches who would invite the personable salesman to demonstrate basketball skills to their teams. He was a deft passer who stressed and demonstrated how to pass into the post. He would challenge players to try to stop his passes and befuddle them with an array of passes, none of which they could stop. They became known as his "invisible passes."[26]

He would also scrimmage against the team stressing the advantages he had because of the shoes he wore. He developed this into the modern basketball clinic. His clinics were demonstrations of his incredible passing ability combined with entertaining trick shots such as a backhanded free throw on one bounce from one end of the court into the basket at the other end.

---

[26] Abraham Aamidor, page 64 of *Chuck Taylor, All Star, The True Story of the Man behind the Most Famous Athletic Shoe in History,* Indiana University Press, 2006

Converse Basketball Yearbook

He developed the Converse Basketball Yearbook in 1922 getting coaches to send pictures of their teams (in their All Stars) with season summaries. It also included articles on basketball skills, game theory and strategy, philosophy, etc., from leading coaches. And, of course, it included testaments on the benefits of Chuck Taylor clinics and their Converse All Star basketball shoes.

Converse All-Americans

Another marketing innovation Chuck started was the selection of All-American players in 1932 for the Converse Yearbook. He would only select players he had personally seen and consulted coaches on his selections using this as a means of access to the coaches who wanted their players to be selected.

As his success increased, so did his territory and he eventually went everywhere in the U.S. developing contacts and conducting clinics from coast to coast. Having Indiana ties helped him as there were Hoosiers everywhere. It is said that he was responsible for getting Everett Case to NC State.

He was the Coach of the Wright Field Army Air Force "Air Tecs", one of, if not the greatest, service basketball teams in history winning 90% of their games against college and other service teams in the 1944-45 season. These games are credited as being one of the greatest influences on the expansion of the popularity of basketball at that time.

There are now basketball clinics and its offspring, basketball camps, all over the world. No one disputes that they improve the skills of the players attending the hundreds of camps. The improvement to the game is magnified as these camps are attended by hundreds of thousands of kids every year.

They also improve the way the game is coached as coaches also improve their coaching skills and learn techniques, drills, etc.

In 1958 he was inducted into the National Sporting Goods Industry Hall of Fame (National Sporting Goods Association). He was honored with selection into the Naismith Hall of Fame in 1969 as a Contributor with one of the most recognized groups ever selected - Red Auerbach, Adolph Rupp, Hank Iba, and Dutch Dehnert. He died later that year with his boyhood dream of basketball immortality realized.

Tony Hinkle (HOF Contributor)

Tony was the president of the National Association of Basketball Coaches (NABC) for 1954–55, and served on their board for many years. He is the person who proposed changing the color of the basketball from dark brown to orange to improve its visibility for both players and fans. He worked with The Spalding Company to come up with a new ball and its trial at the 1958 NCAA Finals in Louisville impressed the NCAA enough that they made it the standard from then on. This innovation improved players by enabling them to see the ball better. This had an even greater impact on fans enjoyment of the game.

He won NABC's top award in 1962 for contributions to the betterment of the game of basketball. He was named Chairman of the Rules Committee of the National Basketball Committee of the U.S. and Canada. He was inducted into the Naismith Memorial Basketball Hall of Fame as a contributor in 1965. He entered the Indiana Basketball Hall of Fame in 1964 and the Indiana Football Hall of Fame in 1974.

Everett Case (HOF Coach)

Case is a Hall of Fame coach who was also an amazing marketer of the game. He brought not only the Indiana style of basketball to North Carolina; but also a flair for presentation.

- **Cutting down the nets**
  Case introduced the fans to the Indiana high school tradition of cutting down the nets after winning a championship that is still done today.

- **Spotlighting Player Introductions**
  He also pioneered shining a spotlight on his players as they were introduced.

- **Post Season Conference Tournaments**
  Case pushed for and got the ACC to have a post season tournament with the winner getting the automatic bid for the NCAA tournament making it a "can't miss" event. The result of this is that there hasn't been a public sale of tickets for it since 1966. And every other Conference now has implemented this event.

- **The 10-second line**
  He is also credited with the use of an official time clock (replacing the use of a stop watch) and the 10-second line.[27] This significantly changed the way the game was played prohibiting teams from stalling all over the court. It also gave coaches the opportunity to devise defenses that would take advantage of the rule. The use of an official time clock helped fans know when the period would end.

- **Filming Games**
  Case was the first coach to film games.[28] It is hard to imagine any innovation that has had a bigger impact on the playing and coaching of basketball. Players study themselves as well as their opponents in preparing for each game. Coaches have staffs of people poring over films to analyze opponents and prepare their team. Play is dissected, diagnosed, and diagrammed by reviewing the films over and over again.

Fans are also rewarded by being able to watch games over and over

---

[27] Indiana Basketball History, Summer, 2013, by Roger Dickinson
[28] *Blue Blood: Duke-Carolina: Inside the Most Storied Rivalry in College Hoops,* By Art Chansky, Dick Vitale, p.52

Arthur L. Trester (HOF Contributor)

Born June 10, 1878, in Hendricks County, Trester became one of the most influential persons in the establishment of "Hoosier Hysteria." He was one of the men responsible for the establishment of the Indiana High School Athletic Association (IHSAA) in 1904 and worked for half of his 66 years to improve the organization until it became a model for other states. When he died in September, 1944, its membership included more than 800 schools. "Called the 'Czar' of Indiana high school athletics, Trester's engaging personality helped high school basketball flourish on a national level."[29]

The Trester Award is one of the highest individual awards in Indiana high School basketball. Named after Arthur Trester, it was established by The IHSAA Board of Control in a written memorial incorporated in the 1945 IHSAA Handbook, that reads:

Arthur L. Trester--a man who had a positive outlook on life, a belief in a fuller and richer philosophy; one who possessed courageous integrity--passing for truth with an unbiased attitude; a personality that reflected dignity, poise, and forcefulness among professional and lay groups; a confidence in the judgments of high school boys and girls and a champion for their educational welfare;--all of which constitutes a philosophy which has contributed to the building of an association which is an integral part of our Indiana secondary school program.

As a partial expression of our high esteem and sincere appreciation of the life of Arthur L. Trester, the Indiana High School Athletic Association establishes this memorial to be known as The Arthur L. Trester Medal for Mental Attitude, this medal to be awarded each year.[30]

Trester was inducted into the Naismith Hall of Fame in 1961 and in the Indiana Basketball Hall of Fame in 1965.

W.R. Clifford "Cliff" Wells (HOF Contributor)

Cliff Wells graduated from Bloomington High School in 1916. Three years after graduating he coached the team to their first state Championship. He was an Indiana high school basketball coach for three decades. He won more than 70% of his games; won more than 50 total tournament sectionals, regionals, semi-states and two state championships; and is the youngest coach to win the state tournament.

He went to Tulane University and coached there from 1946 to 1963 winning 259 games, still the most by any Tulane coach.

His philosophy and approach are best summed up by these quotes:

"I am a firm believer that condition means stamina. Stamina demands training. Training spells sacrifice. Sacrifice is the highway to desire. If a boy is traveling another road he is lost in every sense of the word. I would not have him on my squad."[31]

---

[29] From the Naismith Basketball Hall of Fame at http://www.hoophall.com/hall-of-famers/tag/arthur-l-trester

[30] http://zenas4.tripod.com/orestesindianahistory/id34.html

[31] http://www.tulane.edu/~athletic/mbk/mbkhist/tumbkhistory.html

"The athlete at his best learns something different. Not comfortable ease. Not idleness. Not self-indulgence. Not jaunty contempt for authority. These never win any game. Instead, these: obedience, self-denial, team play and always the inner cry - 'I must, I MUST and I will!' "[32]

Sport Administration

The "Dean of Indiana High School Coaches"[33], he first displayed his outstanding administrative skills as the first president of the Indiana High School Coaches Association.

While at Tulane he served as member of the National Rules Committee from 1952 to 1956. When he retired from Tulane, Wells became the first executive secretary of the National Collegiate Basketball Coaches Association (NABC). He also, served as association president in 1958 and as executive officer in 1966. The Cliff Wells Appreciation Award is presented for outstanding contributions made by an individual to the NABC. He also conducted many clinics and wrote numerous articles on coaching and basketball.

In 1963 he became the first full-time executive secretary and director of the Naismith Memorial Basketball Hall of Fame and served as such until 1966.

Wells was enshrined in the Indiana Basketball Hall of Fame in 1965 and the Naismith Hall of Fame as a Contributor in 1972 as "--coach, administrator, and avid promoter of the game"[34].

---

[32] Ibid.
[33] Ibid.
[34] http://www.hoophall.com/hall-of-famers/tag/wr-clifford-cliff-wells

Additional Supporting Facts

The following are additional facts that demonstrate the strength of Indiana's case as center of the basketball world.

Hoosiers and the ACC

The Atlantic Coast Conference (ACC) is one of the premiere basketball conferences today. Yet few realize that the success of the conference has its roots in Indiana basketball. In fact four transplanted Hoosiers – Everett Case, Eddie Cameron, Vic Bubas and Norm Sloan started the love of basketball now enjoyed by North Carolina fans and the rest of the ACC.

Everett Case: "Father of ACC Basketball"

Everett Case has been called "the father of ACC basketball."[35] He graduated from Anderson High School in 1917 and the University of Wisconsin in 1926. He coached high school basketball in Indiana for 23 years compiling a 726-75 record, an astounding 90% winning percentage and won four Indiana State Championships with Frankfort. He left Indiana to serve in the Navy in World War II and when he returned from the service in 1946, he surprised and disappointed many by eschewing opportunities to coach in his home state and accepted the position of head coach at North Carolina State University.

Basketball was almost an afterthought to most North Carolinians. College football and minor league baseball were the sports most followed. His plan to change all of that was simple – bring Indiana style of play of sound fundamentals, fast break offense and in-your-face defense to North Carolina. He used his legendary status in Indiana to recruit future All-Americans and NBA players Sammy Ranzino (Gary) and Dick Dickey (Pendleton) as well as future ACC coaches Vic Bubas (Gary) and Norm Sloan (Indianapolis).

The results were immediate. The highest point total a Wolfpack team had ever scored before Case's arrival was 71. They topped that five times his first year while increasing their average score by 50%. They ***averaged*** 75 points per game his second year. North Carolina basketball had been changed forever.

Case's basketball had another immediate impact. This was on the fans. The year before Case's arrival few fans watched NC State basketball. The February, 1947, scheduled game between State and UNC had to be cancelled by the Fire Marshall because there were too many fans pouring in any way they could including through restroom windows. SoCon (Southern Conference) officials immediately moved their tournament from its scheduled venue, 3,500 seat Raleigh Auditorium, to Duke's new 9,000 seat Indoor Stadium to meet the surge in ticket requests.

Case's teams dominated the Southern Conference winning the conference title in each of his first six years. In 1953 NC State and the other big schools left the SoCon to start the Atlantic Coast Conference (ACC). He won the first three ACC titles and a fourth in 1958 making him the champion in nine of his first ten years with an overall record of 267-60, an 81.7% winning percentage.

---

[35] http://en.wikipedia.org/wiki/Atlantic_Coast_Conference

His success inspired other schools to upgrade their programs. Case defeated North Carolina fifteen straight times causing UNC to go after St. John's Frank McGuire. Wake Forest went after and hired Bones McKinney and Duke brought in Case protégé and Hoosier Vic Bubas. They all also increased recruiting efforts and upgraded their facilities to compete with the "red menace" at State.

Case is still the all-time winningest coach in North Carolina State history with an overall record of 377-134 (73.7%). He was voted ACC Coach of the Year in 1954, 1955, and 1958. His teams finished 3rd in the 1947 NIT and in the 1950 NCAA Tournament. The ACC Tournament MVP award is named in his honor.

Jim Sumner, curator of sports and recreation for the North Carolina's Museum of History and author of *A History of Sports in North Carolina*, makes the case that Case is the most significant sports personality in North Carolina sports history. He states "Coaching legends like Dean Smith, Mike Krzyzewski and Jim Valvano, and modern-era Big Four All-Americas like David Thompson, Michael Jordan, Grant Hill and Tim Duncan--These, and all the other great ACC players, owe an enormous debt to the man they called "the Old Gray Fox," the man most responsible for turning college basketball into North Carolina's sporting passion."[36]

He was inducted into the Indiana Basketball Hall of Fame in 1962, the North Carolina Sports Hall of Fame in 1964, and the Naismith Memorial Basketball Hall and Helms Foundation Hall of Fame in 1982.

Edmund "Eddie" Cameron

Eddie Cameron was born near Pittsburgh in 1902. He attended Culver Military Academy in Culver, Indiana, where he starred in both football and basketball. He went to Washington & Lee University where he was captain of both the football and basketball teams and tied for the national scoring leader in football his senior season. He stayed at Washington & Lee after graduation to be an assistant to football coach and head basketball coach. He was 8-5 for the 1924-25 season and then went with head football coach, Jimmy DeHart, to Duke to become the freshman football coach. He became backfield coach when Wallace Wade was hired as head coach.

He became head basketball coach in 1928 retaining that position for fourteen years. His success was immediate leading Duke to the finals of the Southern Conference Basketball Tournament in his first two years. His record at Duke was 226-99 (69.5% winning percentage) and 119-56 (68.0% winning percentage) in Southern Conference play. He won conference championships in 1938, 1941 and 1942. His success increased interest in basketball and a new arena was built.

In 1940 Duke finished construction on the 9000 seat Duke Indoor Stadium, the largest basketball venue south of Philadelphia's Palestra. Eddie coached the first game there on January 6, 1940, against Princeton and won 36-27. Thirty-two years later on January 22, 1972, Duke officially changed its name to "Cameron Indoor Arena".

Cameron stepped down from his head basketball coach position to become head football coach in 1942 while Wallace Wade served in World War II. He coached for four years compiling a record of 25-11-1 and winning Duke's first ever bowl game, 29-26, over Alabama in the 1945

---

36 "Who is the Greatest of Them All? Making the Case for Everett Case", by Jim Sumner, <u>Raleigh Metro Magazine,</u> December, 1999, http://www.metronc.com/article/?id=424

Sugar Bowl. When Wade returned in 1946 and resumed the football head coach position, Eddie became permanent Director of Physical Education and Athletics. During this time he helped found the Atlantic Coast Conference and whole heartedly supported Everett Case's drive for the ACC post season basketball tournament to be the means for determining the ACC's automatic bid for the NCAA tournament.

When he retired in 1972, he had the 2nd longest tenure in serving Duke's sports interests. His accomplishments as a player, coach and administrator earned him induction into five Halls of Fame - the National Football, Atlantic Coast Conference Sports Writers, Duke University, North Carolina and Virginia Halls of Fame.

"While Cap Card is credited with introducing basketball in 1905, Eddie Cameron's success built the popularity for the sport as we know it today."[37]

Norm Sloan

Another one of Case's early Indiana recruits was Norm Sloan who graduated from Indianapolis' Lawrence Central in 1944. Upon graduation from NC State, he coached for four years at Presbyterian College where he was 69-36 (66%); then four years at the Citadel. In his first year there he won the George Mikan award for the most improved basketball team. His 57-38 (60%) record there garnered him an offer to coach at Florida.

His six years at Florida were highlighted by their first win ever over an Adolph Rupp coached Kentucky team. He was 85-63 (57%) before returning to his alma mater in 1966. Although his overall record in the fourteen years he piloted the Wolfpack was not quite as impressive as Case's (266-127, 68% winning percentage), he did perform one feat Case never did by winning State's first NCAA Championship in 1974 with Hoosiers Monte Towe and Tim Stoddard supporting future NBA superstar David Thompson. He was selected the National Coach of the Year in 1973 by Basketball Weekly and again in 1974 by the USBWA and the Associated Press.

"Stormin' Norman" went back to Florida in 1980 where he coached the final nine years of his career. He won 53% of his games during this period and won the school's first SEC regular season championship in 1989. His overall record at Florida was 235-194 for a 55% winning percentage and turned the traditional football power into a formidable basketball school.

He is in the Indiana Basketball Hall of Fame (1984) and the North Carolina Sports Hall of Fame (1994).

---

[37] *The Duke Dialog*, March 1, 1996, by William King and reprinted on the internet at http://library.duke.edu/uarchives/history/histnotes/eddie_cameron.html

Vic Bubas

A major key to Case's early success at NC State was his ability to recruit top-flight Indiana talent. One of those recruits was Vic Bubas who graduated from Gary's Lew Wallace High School in 1944. He was twice an All Southern Conference selection and stayed with Case after graduation in 1951 to become freshman coach and then an assistant under Case in 1955.

In 1959, Duke decided to duplicate a little of the Case magic by offering Bubas their head coaching position and Vic accepted. Like Case, his impact was immediate. Despite finishing 4th in ACC regular season, he upset Top-20 ranked teams North Carolina and Wake Forest to win the ACC Tournament and the automatic bid to the NCAA. There he won two games making it to the Elite 8.

He coached for ten years winning 213 games while losing only 67, a 76% winning percentage. His ACC Conference record was 106-32 for a 77% winning percentage. He won 87% of his home games at Duke Indoor Stadium and finished in the AP Top-10 basketball poll in seven of his ten seasons. They made the NCAA Tournament three more times finishing 3rd twice and runner-up once and a 73.33% winning percentage for his NCAA Tournament games. Before Bubas, Duke had one NCAA Tournament appearance and no wins.

He coached five All-Americans, three ACC Players of the Year, twelve 1st Team All-ACC selections and sixteen players drafted by the NBA. Among the assistants he mentored at Duke are Hubie Brown and Chuck Daly.

Vic Bubas learned much from Everett Case. However, he had a whole set of new ideas on one aspect of college coaching – recruiting. Bubas pioneered the process of keeping files on prospective recruits at an early age. He decided that to get an edge on his competition he would start recruiting a player earlier than anyone else. He started sending newspaper articles on Duke basketball before they were seniors so that when he called upon them they already had valuable information about the success his program had both in the conference and in the tournament. He was also an opportunist. When he learned that Frank McGuire had soured on recruit Art Heyman, Bubas stepped him getting the future two-time All-American to come to Duke.

Dean Smith said, "Vic taught us all how to recruit, we had been starting on prospects in the fall of their senior years while Vic was working on them their junior year. For a while, all of us were trying to catch up with him."[38]

Vic's pioneering recruiting tactics have had a huge impact on the sport of college basketball. Entire businesses (scouting services) have evolved. Players are watched in junior high and some sign letters of intent in the 8th grade or sooner. Whether early recruiting is a positive or a negative, there is no doubt it has significantly affected coaches.

Bubas worked relentlessly on recruiting. It eventually caught up with him and he retired from coaching in 1969. He stayed on at Duke as Vice President of Community Relations and later became the first commissioner of the Sun Belt Conference, a position he held for fourteen years.

Bubas was inducted into the National Collegiate Basketball Hall of Fame in 2007, the North Carolina Sports Hall of Fame in 1975 and the Indiana Basketball Hall of Fame in 2002.

---

[38] http://en.wikipedia.org/wiki/Vic_Bubas

Why Indiana is the Center of the Basketball World

High School Gym Size

A statistic that shows the interest of fans in high school basketball is gym size. Of the fifteen largest high school gyms in the United States, thirteen are in Indiana including the six largest.

Largest High School Gymnasiums in the US

Gym	City	State	Capacity
New Castle Fieldhouse	New Castle	Indiana	9,325
John A. Baratto Athletic Center	East Chicago	Indiana	8,296
Lloyd E. Scott Gymnasium	Seymour	Indiana	8,110
Tiernan Center	Richmond	Indiana	8,100
Muncie Fieldhouse	Muncie	Indiana	7,635
Bill Green Athletic Arena	Marion	Indiana	7,560
Alfred J. Loos Fieldhouse	Dallas	Texas	7,500
North Side Gymnasium	Elkhart	Indiana	7,373
"The Wolves' Den" Gym	Michigan City	Indiana	7,304
West Side High School Gym	Gary	Indiana	7,217
Jefferson High School Gym	Lafayette	Indiana	7,200
Southport High School Gym	Southport	Indiana	7,124
"The Hatchet House"	Washington	Indiana	7,090
Memorial Gymnasium	Columbus	Indiana	7,071
Wildcat Den	Chinle	Arizona	7,000

Indiana Basketball Hall of Fame

Indiana has the only state Basketball Hall of Fame. Established in 1962, it is just a few years younger than the Naismith Memorial Basketball Hall of Fame. It opened the museum in New Castle, Indiana, home of the nation's largest high school gymnasium, 35 miles east of Indianapolis in 1990. It publishes Indiana Basketball History, a quarterly magazine that "offers a fascinating look at the traditions of Indiana high school basketball"[39] for a very modest price.

---

[39] http://hoopshall.com/history/

Why Indiana is the Center of the Basketball World

The Indiana High School Basketball Tournament

Another fact is that Indiana has the fourth oldest state high school basketball tournament having played the first one at Indiana University's basketball arena in 1911. Only Illinois (1908), Utah (1908), and Ohio (1909) have older tournaments.

Year of Each State's First High School Basketball Tournament

State	First Tourney	State	First Tourney	State	First Tourney
Ilinois	1908	Kentucky	1918	Alabama	1923
Utah	1908	Oklahoma	1918	Washington	1923
Ohio	1909	Wyoming	1918	Michigan	1925
Indiana	1911	Oregon	1919	Missouri	1925
Montana	1911	Nevada	1920	Maryland	1927
Nebraska	1911	Pennsylvania	1920	Alaska	1929
Arkansas	1912	New Mexico	1921	North Dakota	1933
Iowa	1912	Tennessee	1921	Arizona	1949
Kansas	1912	Texas	1921	Hawaii	1957
South Dakota	1912	Maine	1921	Delaware	1967
Minnesota	1913	Massachusetts	1921	New York	1981
California	1915	Rhode Island	1921	District of Columbia	UN
North Carolina	1915	Colorado	1922	Louisiana	UN
Viginia	1915	Connecticut	1922	Mississippi	UN
West Virginia	1915	Florida	1922	New Jersey	UN
Wisconsin	1916	Georgia	1922		
Idaho	1917	New Hampshire	1922		
South Carolina	1917	Vermont	1922		

The Indiana-Kentucky All Star Game

This series, often called "the world series of high school basketball," began in 1940 and has continued through 2017. It is a two game series played home and home at various sites within Indiana and Kentucky between the high school all-stars selected by each state and led by each state's "Mr. Basketball".

Indiana won the first game 31-29 and has a 95-43 record in the series (68.8%).

Mr. Basketball

Indiana has honored a high school player as Mr. Basketball every year since 1939. It is always given to an outstanding player and is, traditionally, for the "top" player. As there is always heated debate about who is the "top" or "best" player, competition for the title is keen. It is a genuine honor to join a fraternity that includes legends like Oscar Robertson, professional stars such as George McGinnis, Glen Robinson, Greg Oden, Eric Gordon, et.al, and high school legends like Bobby Plumb, Rick Mount, Billy and Dave Shepherd, etc. It is an honor that even Larry Bird does not have (no state is perfect). The honor is selected by the Indianapolis Star newspaper.

The Table below lists every Indiana Mr. Basketball with the high school and college they attended in sequence by year. Players notated with an '*' are the 22 Mr. Basketballs who went on to play in the NBA or the ABA.

Why Indiana is the Center of the Basketball World

Twenty-six Mr. Basketballs have gone to Indiana University; ten to Purdue; four to Kentucky; and three each to North Carolina, Ohio State, Cincinnati and Miami (OH). Only two have gone to Notre Dame and two did not go on to college (1941 & 1950). The last Mr. Basketball to go to Purdue was Caleb Swanigan in 2015. Two of three Mr. Basketballs that have gone to Ohio State and North Carolina have been this decade.

The first Mr. Basketball was George Crowe from Franklin in 1939. "Although segregation was a fact of life in 1930's, Indiana took a giant leap forward by selecting Crowe, a gifted black athlete, as its first Mr. Basketball."[40] Crowe was also a gifted baseball player and was one of the early African-Americans to play in the major leagues from 1952 – 1961. When he retired he had the record for most pinch hit home runs.

In 1950 Pat Klein was the first person to be selected Mr. Basketball and win the Trester award. He is one of only two Mr. Basketballs who did not go to college. Upon graduation from Marion he enlisted in the Navy. Hallie Bryant (1953) starred at IU and then played with the Globetrotters. The Van Arsdale twins (Tom and Dick) were the first Co-Mr. Basketballs selected (1961). Both had 12 year NBA careers after starring at IU. Dick Van Arsdale was the first member of the Phoenix Suns.[41] Co-Mr. Basketballs were also awarded in 1974, 1984, and 1987.

---

[40] Indianapolis Monthly, March, 1995, p. 105 and reprinted at
http://books.google.com/books?id=RuoCAAAAMBAJ&pg=PA105#v=onepage&q&f=false
[41] Ibid., p.111

Why Indiana is the Center of the Basketball World

Indiana Mr. Basketball by Year

Year	Player	High School	College
1939	George Crowe	Franklin	Indiana Central
1940	Ed Schienbein	Southport	Indiana
1941	John Bass	Greenwood	
1942	Bud Brown	Muncie Burris	Georgetown
1943	None	World War II	
1944	None	World War II	
1945	Tom Schwartz	Kokomo	Indiana
1946	Johnny Wilson	Anderson	Anderson
1947	Bill Garrett	Shelbyville	Indiana
1948	Bob Masters	Lafayette Jefferson	Indiana
1949	Dee Monroe	Madison	Kentucky
1950	Pat Klein	Marion	
1951	Tom Harold	Muncie Central	Colorado
1952	Joe Sexson	Indianapolis Tech	Purdue
1953	Hallie Bryant	Crispus Attucks	Indiana
1954	Bobby Plump	Milan	Butler
1955	Wilson Eison	Gary Roosevelt	Purdue
1956	Oscar Robertson*	Crispus Attucks	Cincinnati
1957	John Coalman	South Bend Central	Fordham
1958	Mike McCoy	Ft. Wayne South Side	Miami (OH)
1959	Jimmy Rayl*	Kokomo	Indiana
1960	Ron Bonham*	Muncie Central	Cincinnati
1961	Tom Van Arsdale'	Indianapolis Manual	Indiana
	Dick Van Arsdale'	Indianapolis Manual	Indiana
1962	Larry Humes	Madison	Evansville
1963	Rick Jones	Muncie Central	Miami (OH)
1964	Dennis Brady	Lafayette Jefferson	Purdue
1965	Billy Keller*	Indianapolis Washington	Purdue
1966	Rick Mount*	Lebanon	Purdue
1967	Willie Long*	Ft. Wayne South Side	New Mexico
1968	Billy Shepherd*	Carmel	Butler
1969	George McGinnis'	Indianapolis Washington	Indiana
1970	Dave Sheperd	Carmel	Indiana
1971	Mike Flynn*	Jeffersonville	Kentucky
1972	Phil Cox	Connersville	Gardner-Webb
1973	Kent Benson	New Castle	Indiana
1974	Steve Collier	Southwestern	Cincinnati
	Roy Taylor	Anderson	Youngstown State
1975	Kyle Macy*	Peru	Purdue
1976	Dave Colescott	Marion	North Carolina
1977	Ray Tolbert*	Madison Heights	Indiana
1978	David Magley*	South Bend LaSalle	Kansas

Year	Player	High School	College
1979	Steve Bouchie	Washington	Indiana
1980	Jim Master	Ft. Wayne Harding	Kentucky
1981	Dan Palombizio	Michigan City Rogers	Purdue, Ball State
1982	Roger Harden	Valparaiso	Kentucky
1983	Steve Alford*	New Castle	Indiana
1984	Delray Brooks	Michigan City Rogers	Indiana, Providence
	Troy Lewis	Anderson	Purdue
1985	Jeff Grose	Warsaw	Northwestern
1986	Mark Jewell	Lafayette Jefferson	Evansville
1987	Jay Edwards*	Marion	Indiana
	Lyndon Jones	Marion	Indiana
1988	Woody Austin	Richmond	Purdue
1989	Pat Graham	Floyd Central	Indiana
1990	Damon Bailey	Bedford North Lawrence	Indiana
1991	Glenn Robinson*	Gary Roosevelt	Purdue
1992	Charles Macon	Michigan City Elston	Ohio State
1993	Maurice Fuller	Anderson	Southern
1994	Bryce Drew*	Valparaiso	Valparaiso
1995	Damon Frierson	Ben Davis	Miami (OH)
1996	Kevin Ault	Warsaw	Missouri State
1997	Luke Recker	DeKalb	Indiana, Iowa
1998	Tom Coverdale	Noblesville	Indiana
1999	Jason Gardner	Indianapolis North Central	Arizona
2000	Jared Jeffries*	Bloomington North	Indiana
2001	Chris Thomas	Indianapolis Pike	Notre Dame
2002	Sean May*	Bloomington North	North Carolina
2003	Justin Cage	Indianapolis Pike	Xavier
2004	A.J. Ratliff	Indianapolis North Central	Indiana
2005	Luke Zeller*	Washington	Notre Dame
2006	Greg Oden*	Lawrence North	Ohio State
2007	Eric Gordon*	Indianapolis North Central	Indiana
2008	Tyler Zeller*	Washington	North Carolina
2009	Jordan Hulls	Bloomington South	Indiana
2010	Deshaun Thomas	Bishop Luers	Ohio State
2011	Cody Zeller*	Washington	Indiana
2012	Gary Harris*	Hamilton Southeastern	Michigan State
2013	Zak Irvin	Hamilton Southeastern	Michigan
2014	Trey Lyles*	Arsenal Tecnical	Kentucky
2015	Caleb Swanigan	Homestead	Purdue
2016	Kyle Guy	Lawrence Central	Virginia
2017	Kris Wilkes	Indpls North Central	UCLA

The Most Famous High School Teams in History

Indiana can also claim to have the two most famous high school basketball teams in history. Milan's 1954 state championship has been immortalized by the movie *Hoosiers* and Franklin's "Wonder Five" is still considered the best high school basketball team ever produced in Indiana.

The 1954 Milan State Champions

The most recognized High School basketball team in history is the 1954 Milan, Indiana, team that with a total student enrollment 161 won the state championship. The team came close in 1953 to making the Final 4, but were squashed by South Bend Central 56-37 in the afternoon semifinal.

Led by returning star Bobby Plump, the '54 team made it out of the Indianapolis semi-state by defeating an even smaller school – Montezuma with a total enrollment of 79 before facing Oscar Robertson's Crispus Attucks team in the semi-state final. Milan played a masterful game after getting ahead by seven in the 2nd quarter. No shot clock was in effect so Milan passed the ball around until they got a lay-up or an open shot for Plump and surprised the talented Attucks team 65-52.

They defeated Terre Haute Gerstmeyer in the afternoon game of the Finals at Hinkle Fieldhouse in a much easier than anticipated 60-48 game. They had to beat a heavily favored Muncie Central team that had been 23-5 going into the Final game. With the game tied and 4 minutes to play and Milan's star held to 2 for 10 shooting, they held the ball for a final shot. Plump took the historic shot with time running out to propel Milan into the ranks of superstardom and the Indiana State Championship.

It is estimated that as many as 40,000 people celebrated with the 1120 residents of Milan the next day lining the road into Milan for 13 miles.

A museum has been opened that memorializes Milan team. Information can be viewed at their website: http://www.milan54.org/.

The Franklin "Wonder Five"

No team in Indiana basketball history was as successful as Franklin's "Wonder Five." They grew up together in small Franklin, Indiana, playing basketball and getting to know each other as well as any team at any time. Burl Friddle, Ralph Hicks, Paul White, Robert "Fuzzy" Vandivier, Sima Comer, Johnny "Snake Eyes" Gant, Harold Borden, and Pete Keeling played together in high school compiling a four year record of 104-10, an astonishing 91.2% winning percentage, winning three consecutive state championships in 1920, '21 and '22.

Then the core of the team, including coach Ernest "Griz" Wagner, went to Franklin College and in 1923 went undefeated including wins over Purdue, Illinois, Wisconsin and Notre Dame as well as two games against the professional team from Detroit. They were named the national champion in 1923 and continued to be undefeated winning 50 consecutive games until 1924 when Tony Hinkle's "Giant Killers," Butler, handed them their first loss. The *Detroit Free Press* wrote: "Not only has this team been the best Franklin College ever had, but it is considered as the best collegiate team ever seen in Hoosierdom, the basketball center of the world."[42]

Fuzzy Vandivier was named by the Chicago Tribunes as one of the five best players in the country and John Wooden thought he was the finest high school player he had ever seen.[43]

Their success led the high school to change its nickname to the "Grizzly Cubs" and the college to the "Grizzly Bears" in honor of the coach. Their success was chronicled in the 1986 book *The Franklin Wonder Five: A Complete History of the Legendary Basketball Team*, by Phillip Ellett published by RLE Enterprises.

Vandivier (1962), Gant (1967), Friddle (1969) and Coach Wagner (1962) have been inducted into the Indiana Basketball Hall of Fame. Fuzzy Vandivier was inducted into the Naismith Basketball Hall of Fame and Helms Foundation Hall of Fame in 1975.

Robert Montgomery "Bob" Knight

Although not a Hoosier, no one is more associated with Indiana basketball than Bob Knight. Born in Massillon, Ohio, on October 25, 1940, and raised in nearby Orrville, Knight was a star in high school in both football and basketball graduating in 1958. He went to Ohio State and played as the sixth man on the 1960 national championship team with future NBA stars and Hall of Famers John Havlicek and Jerry Lucas. He also played football at OSU for legendary coach and personality Woody Hayes.

He graduated from Ohio State in 1962 with a degree in history and government. After coaching a high school junior varsity team for one year, Knight enlisted in the Army. He became the assistant coach at Army in 1963 and head coach in 1965. Despite the size limitations the Army put on their recruits (6' 5"), Knight's Cadets won 102 of the 152 games he coached over a six year period for a 67.1% winning percentage. He went to the NIT four times gaining the semi-finals three times.

In 1970 Minnesota interviewed the young "Bobby" Knight to replace Bill Fitch but decided to promote Fitch's assistant, George Hanson. Hanson resigned the following year and Minnesota called Knight to see if he was still interested. For a second time in their history they were too late to sign a future coaching legend as Knight had just accepted IU's head coaching position.

Over the next twenty-nine years Knight won 661 and lost only 240 games for a 73.3% winning percentage. He won 353 Big Ten games (conference best) and lost only 151, a (70.0%) He won or tied for eleven Big Ten Championships (tied for conference best); finished 2nd five times; never had a losing season; had only two losing Big Ten seasons; had two undefeated Big Ten seasons; and is the last coach to go undefeated for an entire season. His IU teams made the NCAA tournament twenty-five times; made the Final 4 five times; won three national championships; and had one third place finish.

Knight finished his coaching career at Texas Tech winning 138 games out of 220, (62.7%) and 53 of 102 Big 12 conference games (51.9%). His Red Raiders went to the NCAA four times and the NIT once in his six full seasons. He retired in the middle of his seventh season handing over

---

[42] http://en.wikipedia.org/wiki/Franklin_Wonder_Five
[43] Ibid.

the reins to his son Pat. His twenty-eight NCAA Tournament appearances is the most of any coach tied with Lute Olsen.

There is no doubt that many of the incidents that have been cataloged about Coach Knight would be considered unacceptable behaviors by many, possibly most people and universities. Yet Knight was able to weather them up until the end. Only in Indiana could he have lasted as long as he did. Only in Indiana would 4,000 people have come out to protest his firing and that many, many more would protest in letters and editorials. And I don't think it was the winning that inspired his admirers. It was the integrity of his program and, mostly, the absolute purity and beauty of the way his teams played basketball.

You can be critical of his personality. You can be embarrassed as a Hoosier or an IU alum by some of his antics. But only a basketball moron would not absolutely love to watch his teams play.

Additional Trivia

"Hoosiers"

The 1954 Milan season was fictionalized in the 1986 movie hit *"Hoosiers"* that starred Academy Award winning actor Gene Hackman. Written by Bloomington native and IU grad Angelo Pizzo and directed by David Anspaugh, a fraternity brother of Pizzo's at IU, the movie is about a 1951/52 small Indiana school's run to the Indiana high school championship.

The movie focuses on Hackman's character who was a successful college coach banned from coaching after physically accosting one of his players. It does mirror the 1954 Milan team in two distinct ways. The Milan coach, Marvin Wood portrayed by Hackman as Norman Dale in the movie, did close practices to the townspeople creating the uproar. And Jimmy Chitwood's final shot in the championship game was choreographed exactly to Plump's final shot in Milan's victory although in the movie they did not hold the ball for the final four minutes.

The movie successfully captured the fervor and passion that small towns had for their basketball and won two Academy Award nominations. Dennis Hopper was nominated for Best Supporting Actor and the music score garnered a nomination for Jerry Goldsmith. It is generally accepted as the best basketball movie ever by every major sports publication[44] and has been selected as the best sports movie ever by a number of publications. The American Film Institute rates it the 4th best Sports Movie of all time[45] and the 13th most inspirational film of all time[46].

NBA Coaches Trivia Question:

Who are the two former NBA coaches who each:

- Were born in Indiana in 1937
- Graduated from Indiana high schools in 1955
- Graduated from non-Division I colleges
- Began their coaching careers at Indiana high schools
- Coached college basketball for 8+ seasons before coaching in the NBA
- Coached 14 or more NBA seasons
- Coached two Western Conference teams and one Eastern Conference team
- Coached more than 1000 regular season NBA games
- Won more than 51% of their regular season games
- Coached in 11 NBA Playoffs
- Coached in the NBA Finals only once and were defeated by the Boston Celtics

Answer: Del Harris and John MacLeod

---

[44] The exception is Sports Illustrated who picks it as the 2nd best basketball movie just to be different.
[45] http://www.comingsoon.net/news/movienews.php?id=46072
[46] http://connect.afi.com/site/DocServer/cheers100.pdf?docID=202

Why Indiana is the Center of the Basketball World

Oh! What a Night!

I was fortunate to play basketball at Carmel for former Indiana Hall of Fame coaches Bill Shepherd and Eric Clark; and with two Mr. Basketballs, Billy and Dave Shepherd. I was also privileged to be on the floor when one of the most spectacular performances on a basketball floor by anyone at any time occurred.

On Saturday, January 6, 1968, Billy exploded for *70* points. Brownsburg was the unfortunate recipient of his amazing feat. They were not a bad team and, in fact, were one of the sixty-four teams that won their sectional that year. They were just in the wrong place at the wrong time.

On the preceding night Kent Carson broke the Hamilton County record for points in a game by scoring 52. The hotshot from Hamilton Heights' record inspired Billy and at half time of our game, Billy had 24. Coach Shepherd asked us if we wanted Billy go for Carson's record. We weren't happy that Kent had the record and were unanimous and enthusiastic with our approval. We went out in the second half absolutely determined to help him get the record. He scored an incredible forty-six points in the 2nd half hitting shots from everywhere. At least half of his baskets were outside today's NBA three point line.

To put Billy's feat into some perspective, when Wilt Chamberlain scored 100 points to set the record for an NBA game, he scored at a rate of 2.08 points per minute. Billy scored 2.19 points per minute and had the three point field goal been in effect, his rate would have been 2.65 to 2.81 points per minute.

Another interesting statistic that demonstrates how hot he was that night is that for the year Billy averaged 33 points per game and the rest of the team combined averaged 48.5 points per game. In that game we scored 47 of the 117 points or 97% of our average while Billy more than doubled his average.

Billy played three years in the ABA with the Virginia Squires (72/73), San Diego Conquistadors (73/74, under head coach Wilt Chamberlain), and Memphis Sounds (74/75). He holds the ABA's single season record for three point field goal accuracy set in the 1974-75 season.

Dave Shepherd: How to Follow a Legend!

OK. No pressure. Your school had not won a Sectional in 40 years before your brother (1968 Mr. Basketball) hit a buzzer beater and the town went crazy. They hadn't lost one since. *How do you follow that?*

First, as a Junior, you have an undefeated regular season. Then, as a Senior, you lead your team to the Final Game of the State Tournament, break Oscar Robertson's Final Game scoring record, and set what is still the single season scoring record! Oh, yeah. You are selected as Indiana's Mr. Basketball.

Shoe Bomber Hero

Kwame James (no relation to Lebron or Lester) is a graduate of Indianapolis Lawrence North High School and Evansville University. He was dozing during his December 22, 2001, flight from Paris to Miami when a flight attendant awakened him to a disturbance a few rows back. Richard Reid was attempting to detonate a bomb he had in his shoes. The flight attendants were not able to completely subdue the 6'4" Reid and asked Kwame for assistance. The 6' 8" center helped tie up Reid with belts and headset wires, and took turns holding Reid by his ponytail with another passenger for the remainder of the flight until making an emergency landing in Boston.

The "Epitome of Cool"[47]

How cool is Indiana high school basketball? James Dean played at Fairmount High School. He was born February 8, 1931, in Marion, In. He moved with his family to California in 1937 but moved back to Fairmount, Indiana, in 1938 to live with his grandparents after the death of his mother. He played baseball and was a three year starter on the basketball team.

There is no doubt he was a star. In his senior season he led the team in their Sectional to wins over two schools who had beaten Fairmount during the season and that he scored 15 of his team's 34 points in their loss to powerhouse Marion in the final game.

His legend was expanded in the October 13, 1955, *Fairmount News* notice of his death, to have hit a last second shot to beat Gas City. However, Gas City didn't exist in 1949 having been absorbed in consolidation that formed Mississinewa High School, who Fairmount beat in the semifinals. However, local newspaper recaps of the games relate how well he played but do not mention any last second heroics.

The legends of persons like James Dean are often enhanced with stories that are sometimes embellishments of the facts. It is completely in character for one of these coming from Indiana to be about basketball.

Where else could something like this happen but in Indiana?[48]

In June, 1977, the Indiana Pacers were broke and looked like they wouldn't make it to their 2nd season in the NBA. The $3.2 million entry fee plus the compensation promised to the ABA teams not accepted by the NBA drained the coffers of owner and local businessman Bob Eason. With no NBA television revenue coming for three more years, the financial situation was dire.

Coach Bobby Leonard and his wife Nancy were on vacation in Hawaii when they were told the Pacers would probably be sold and moved by the end of July. They immediately flew home and met with the owners, TV and radio broadcasters, and others to determine how to save the franchise. They needed $2 million or 8000 season ticket purchases and needed it immediately.

It's unclear who first suggested the idea for a telethon, but it's clear that Nancy Leonard, the first female General Manager of any professional sport, pounced on it. In just a few days they outfitted the '500' Ballroom of the Indiana Convention Center with tables, chairs, and telephones for the volunteers, including Pacer star Billy Knight, to take season ticket orders.

On the evening of July 3, WTTV-4 went on the air live with 1070 WIBC radio broadcasting the Save-the-Pacer telethon. For 16.5 hours Bobby and Nancy updated the public with their progress. WRTV (Channel 6) and WTHR (Channel 13) aired major portions of the telethon. People who could not afford season tickets sent $1, $5, $10, whatever they could. Children went door-to-door collecting pennies, nickels, dimes, quarters, however much people would contribute. In total $30,000 in donations was raised. Things were looking good.

An hour and a half before the end, Bobby announced that a miscalculation of 822 seats raised the total needed from just 475 to 1300 in a very short time. It didn't look good. At 10 minutes before the end, Nancy in tears told Bobby, "We're at 8028." The people of Indiana had saved the Pacers.

---

[47] http://articles.latimes.com/2010/sep/30/opinion/la-oe-oneill-jamesdean-20100930

[48] WTTV executive producer Peggy McClelland http://www.indystar.com/story/sports/nba/pacers/2016/02/17/1977-telethon-magical-chapter-pacers-fairy-tale-story/80498674/

Now You Know !

1. Indiana has the highest concentration of coaches in NCAA Division I history
2. Indiana has the highest concentration of consensus All-Americans in NCAA Division I history
3. Indiana has the highest concentration of players in NBA history
4. Indiana has the highest concentration of coaches in NBA history
5. The six largest and thirteen of the fourteen largest high school gymnasiums are in Indiana
6. The most famous high school basketball team in history is Milan's 1954 State Champion team
7. John Wooden was selected as the best coach of any sport in history
8. Tony Hinkle invented the orange basketball
9. Piggy Lambert developed the fast break style of basketball
10. Vic Bubas developed the recruiting process used by most college coaches today
11. Chuck Taylor developed the first basketball shoe
12. In 1919 Elmer Oliphant developed the intramural system that is used today
13. Everett Case, Eddie Cameron, Vic Bubas and Norm Sloan are largely responsible for the ACC becoming the basketball power conference it is today
14. John Wooden is the most successful coach in NCAA Tournament history
15. Clyde Lovellette is the only person to lead the NCAA in scoring and win the NCAA Championship in the same year
16. Chuck Taylor developed the first basketball clinic
17. Oscar Robertson is largely responsible for free agency in the NBA
18. Larry Bird is largely responsible for expanding the NBA's salary cap rules
19. John Wooden was the first person inducted into the Naismith Basketball Hall of Fame as a player and a coach
20. Cliff Wells was the first Executive Director of the Naismith Hall of Fame
21. Louie Dampier is the ABA's career leader in pointes and assists
22. Everett Case is responsible for establishing the first college post season conference tournament that determines the automatic bid to the NCAA tournament
23. Hoosiers John Wooden and Oscar Robertson were two of the first five people voted into the initial class of the College Basketball Hall of Fame
24. In 1960 Hoosiers John Wooden, Stretch Murphy and Branch McCracken along with Victor Hanson and Ed McCauley joined George Mikan (1959 inductee) as the first six Player inductees.
25. James Dean, the "epitome of cool" played for Fairmount High School
26. Indiana is the only state with a population under 10 million to have produced at least three players in every season of the NBA
27. Branch McCracken was the first coach to recruit an African-American in the Big Ten
28. Clyde Lovellette is the only person to win championships with both the Lakers and the Celtics
29. The University of Minnesota barely missed opportunities to hire John Wooden and Bob Knight
30. Everett Case was the first coach to film his games
31. Duke's Cameron Indoor Arena is named for Eddie Cameron, a Culver graduate.
32. Indiana is the only state to have a state-wide high school basketball Hall of Fame
33. Everett Case is responsible for the use of an official time clock
34. "Hoosiers" is considered the best basketball movie ever made
35. Naismith called Indiana "the center of the sport" he invented.
36. Branch McCracken is the only coach at Ball State to beat IU.
37. Everett Dean in his only appearance in the NCAA Tournament coached Stanford to their only National Championship in 1942.
38. The only person in the history of the NBA to be MVP, Coach of the Year and Executive of the year is Larry Bird
39. The Indiana Pacers were the only ABA team to play in all nine seasons and be absorbed by the NBA.
40. Everett Case is responsible for the establishment of the 10 second line
41. Elmer Oliphant was selected as an All-American from Purdue in 1914 and from Army in 1915

Acknowledgements

I would especially like to thank the Indiana Basketball Hall of Fame, New Castle, Indiana, for letting me view their archives and for providing their knowledge and their website Hoopshall.com.

The following sources of information were also used for this analysis:

The Indiana High School Athletic Association and their website
(http://www.ihsaa.org/dnn/Home/tabid/38/Default.aspx)

NBA.com

Basketball-reference.com

Databasebasketball.com

Wikipedia.com

ESPN.com

CBSSports.com

Association for Professional Basketball Research (http://www.apbr.org/apbr-faq.html)

The Indiana High School Basketball History website (http://ww2.usppp.com/unlocks/Default.htm)

Indiana Basketball History, published by the Indiana Basketball Hall of Fame

The James Dean Gallery, Fairmount, IN

Content of Tables

SO-1: Displays the concentrations of the players from each state that entered the NBA in each decade. For each state it shows Pop(M), #, and Con: the population in millions, the number of players from the state, and the concentration, respectively. For each decade it also shows % - the percentage of the state's players that entered that decade. Pop (M) for All Years is the average population between 1930 and 2010. Pop (M) for each decade is the average population for that decade.

SO-2: Displays the concentrations of the players from each state who played a total number of games in the NBA in ranges starting with at 100+ to 1000+ games. For each state it shows Pop(M), #, and Con: the population in millions, the number of coaches from the state, and the concentration, respectively. For each range it also shows % - the percentage of the state's players that played at least that many games. Pop (M) is the average population for the US between 1930 and 2010.

SO-3: Displays the concentrations of the players from each state that played in the ABA. For each state it shows Pop(M), # Players, Con, #NBA Players, and % NBA Players: the population in millions, the number of players from the state, the concentration, the number of players who played in the NBA, and the percentage of players who played in the NBA, respectively.

SO-4: Displays the concentrations of the Number of All-American Selections and the Number of All-American Players from each state for time periods from 1905 through the most recent year (2017). For each state for the Number of Selections it shows Pop (M), #, and Con: the population in millions, the number of selections from the state, and the concentration, respectively. For each state for the Number of Players it shows Pop (M), # and Con: the population in millions, the number of players from the state, and the concentration, respectively. For each time period for both it also shows % - the percentage of the state's selections/players for that time period. Pop (M) for All Years is the average population between 1900 and 2010. Pop (M) for each time period is the average population for that time period.

SO-6: Displays the concentrations of the NBA coaches from each state that began coaching in each decade. For each state it shows Pop (M), #, and Con: the population in millions, the number of coaches from the state, and the concentration, respectively. For each decade it also shows %: the percentage of the state's coaches that entered that decade. Pop (M) for All Years is the average population 1930 and 2010. Pop (M) for each decade is the average population for that decade.

SO-5: Displays the concentrations of the coaches from each state who coached a total number of games in the NBA in ranges starting with at 1+ to 1000+ games. For each state it shows Pop (M), #, and Con: the population in millions, the number of coaches from the state, and the concentration, respectively. For each range it also shows %: the percentage of the state's players that played at least that many games. Pop (M) is the average population between 1930 and 2010.

SO-8: Displays the concentrations of the NCAA coaches from each state that began coaching in periods from 1895 to the present (2017). For each state it shows Pop(M), # and Con: the population in millions, the number of coaches from the state, and the concentration, respectively. For each time period it also shows %: the percentage of the state's players that entered that decade. Pop (M) for All Years is the average population between 1900 and 2010. Pop (M) for each decade is the average population for that time period.

SO-9: Displays the concentrations of the coaches from each state who coached a total number of games in the NCAA in ranges starting with at 100+ to 1000+ games. For each state it shows Pop (M), #, and Con: the population in millions, the number of coaches from the state, and the concentration, respectively. For each range it also shows %: the percentage of the state's players that played at least that many games. Pop (M) is the average population between 1900 and 2010.

SO-HOF: Displays the concentrations of all persons inducted into the Naismith Basketball Hall of Fame as well as the concentrations for the Players, Coaches, and Contributors categories. For each category it shows for each state Pop (M), #, and Con: the population in millions, the number of coaches from the state, and the concentration, respectively.

SO-NBA PLAYERS: Displays the Career stats of the 172 NBA players from Indiana. Players with an "*" are Hall-of-Famers.

SO-AA: Lists all the All-Americans from Indiana selected including year selected and school attended.

SO-NBA COACHES: Displays the Career stats of the 29 NBA coaches from Indiana.

SO-NCAA COACHES: Displays the Career stats of the 107 NCAA coaches from Indiana. Coaches with an "*" are Hall-of-Famers.

SO-1: Concentration of NBA Players by Decade

All Years				1936-1949					1950-1959					1960-1969				
State	Pop (M)	#	Con	State	Pop (M)	#	Con	%	State	Pop (M)	#	Con	Con	State	Pop (M)	#	Con	%
IN	5.149	172	33.403	IN	3.690	39	10.569	23%	IN	4.315	22	5.099	13%	KY	3.134	17	5.424	17%
KY	3.509	98	27.930	UT	2.970	6	9.631	29%	KY	3.002	14	4.664	14%	IN	4.936	19	3.849	11%
MS	2.470	68	27.527	KY	2.902	21	7.238	21%	NY	15.829	52	3.285	14%	LA	3.458	11	3.181	12%
MD	4.303	118	27.420	NY	14.155	80	5.652	21%	PA	10.921	32	2.930	14%	OH	10.198	28	2.746	15%
LA	3.679	91	24.738	IL	8.305	37	4.455	14%	IL	9.413	27	2.869	11%	PA	11.572	28	2.420	13%
IL	10.867	257	23.650	MN	2.894	12	4.147	24%	MO	4.139	9	2.175	15%	MD	3.900	9	2.308	8%
NY	17.230	375	21.764	CO	1.230	5	4.065	16%	CA	13.218	27	2.043	6%	MI	8.365	18	2.152	11%
GA	5.821	122	20.957	PA	10.199	40	3.922	18%	NJ	5.480	11	2.007	8%	TN	3.750	8	2.134	10%
MI	8.346	170	20.369	NJ	4.510	16	3.548	12%	MN	3.211	6	1.869	12%	NC	4.824	10	2.073	8%
NJ	6.860	139	20.261	OH	7.428	26	3.501	14%	OH	8.843	16	1.809	9%	MO	4.505	9	1.998	15%
NC	6.087	119	19.549	CA	8.747	25	2.858	6%	WA	3.707	4	1.525	6%	NY	17.534	34	1.939	9%
CA	22.620	442	19.540	KS	1.858	5	2.691	15%	VA	4.014	6	1.495	6%	MS	2.199	4	1.819	6%
PA	11.575	223	19.266	OK	2.265	6	2.650	13%	KS	2.047	3	1.466	9%	NJ	6.635	11	1.658	8%
VA	5.588	105	18.789	TX	7.082	17	2.401	9%	OK	2.263	3	1.326	7%	OK	2.446	4	1.635	9%
OH	9.997	185	18.506	WI	1.984	7	2.125	12%	CO	1.548	2	1.292	6%	AR	1.856	3	1.617	9%
TN	4.479	79	17.639	IA	2.580	5	1.938	21%	UT	3.620	1	1.256	5%	IL	10.612	17	1.602	7%
AL	3.754	65	17.316	LA	2.533	4	1.579	4%	TN	3.439	4	1.163	5%	OR	1.933	3	1.552	10%
WA	4.489	65	15.863	MO	3.866	6	1.552	10%	MI	7.135	8	1.121	5%	CA	17.911	27	1.507	6%
OK	2.879	45	15.631	WA	3.294	3	1.456	5%	WI	1.932	4	1.079	7%	NE	1.450	2	1.380	18%
AR	2.251	34	15.105	MA	4.504	6	1.332	11%	LA	2.986	3	1.005	3%	VA	4.694	6	1.278	6%
KS	2.332	34	14.580	MI	5.839	7	1.199	4%	AZ	1.037	1	0.964	4%	FL	5.871	7	1.192	6%
CT	2.848	41	14.397	NC	3.816	4	1.048	3%	CT	2.278	2	0.878	5%	GA	4.269	5	1.171	4%
UT	5.248	21	14.078	TN	3.110	3	0.965	4%	NC	4.312	3	0.696	3%	MA	5.428	6	1.105	11%
TX	14.515	186	12.814	VA	3.339	2.5	0.749	1%	MD	3.140	2	0.637	2%	CO	1.984	2	1.008	6%
WI	1.873	57	12.699	MD	2.468	1.5	0.608	1%	OR	1.653	1	0.605	3%	KS	2.214	2	0.904	6%
MN	4.005	50	12.484	CT	1.858	1	0.538	2%	TX	8.683	5	0.576	3%	AL	3.359	3	0.893	5%
MO	4.844	60	12.387	AR	1.928	1	0.519	3%	MS	2.175	1	0.460	1%	TX	10.408	8	0.769	4%
OR	2.452	29	11.826	AL	2.947	1	0.339	2%	SC	2.256	1	0.443	4%	WA	4.191	2	0.638	3%
FL	9.560	110	11.507	GA	3.288	1	0.304	1%	AL	3.167	1	0.316	2%	CT	2.790	1	0.358	2%
CO	2.833	32	11.294	FL	2.359				FL	3.886	1	0.257	1%	IA	2.793	1	0.358	4%
MA	5.595	55	9.831	MS	2.177				MA	4.929	1	0.203	2%	MN	3.616	1	0.277	2%
IA	2.811	24	8.537	NE	1.320				AR	1.847				WI	1.801	1	0.239	2%
AZ	2.967	24	8.088	OR	1.311				GA	3.700				AZ	1.547			
SC	3.099	25	8.066	SC	2.010				IA	2.691				SC	2.492			
NE	1.539	11	7.148	VT	2.061				NE	1.369				UT	4.315			
NM	1.260	8	6.351						VT	2.623				VT	3.137			
ME	1.091			WY	0.272	5	18.416	63%										
VT	4.098			RI	0.746	4	5.362	40%	WY	0.312	2	6.410	25%	DC	0.760	8	10.533	17%
DC	0.680	48	70.553	MT	0.579	2	3.457	33%	WV	0.312	7	3.624	30%	WV	0.332	4	2.222	17%
WY	0.405	8	19.755	NM	0.610	2	3.281	25%	DC	0.788	2	2.538	4%	ND	0.626	1	1.597	33%
NV	1.049	14	13.344	AZ	0.628	2	3.187	8%	NH	0.570	1	1.754	13%	NM	0.988	1	1.013	13%
WV	0.405	23	12.279	HI	0.491	1	2.037	100%	MT	0.638	1	1.567	17%	AK	0.266			
RI	0.919	10	10.876	NH	0.512	1	1.955	13%	AK	0.183				DE	0.499			
NH	0.880	8	9.089	SD	0.648	1	1.544	25%	DE	0.385				HI	0.706			
DE	0.579	5	8.639	WV	0.272	3	1.512	13%	HI	0.567				ID	0.692			
MT	0.760	6	7.895	DC	0.739	1	1.354	2%	ID	0.632				ME	0.984			
AK	0.396	3	7.582	AK	0.138				ME	0.943				MT	0.686			
SD	0.707	4	5.659	DE	0.294				ND	0.625				NH	0.674			
ND	0.640	3	4.685	ID	0.559				NM	0.823				NV	0.389			
ID	0.946	4	4.229	ME	0.879				NV	0.225				RI	0.904			
HI	0.893	1	1.120	ND	0.629				RI	0.818				SD	0.674			
XX		313		NV	0.136				SD	0.667				WY	0.332			
				XX		5		2%	XX					XX				
TOT	223.3	4141	18.544	TOT	144.67	414	2.967	10%	TOT	169.3	284	1.678	6%	TOT	195.627	313	1.600	8%

SO-1: Concentration of NBA Players by Decade

1970-1979

State	Pop (M)	#	Con	%
MS	2.369	19	8.022	28%
IN	5.343	26	4.866	15%
KY	3.441	15	4.359	15%
AL	3.668	15	4.090	23%
MI	9.071	36	3.969	21%
NC	5.479	21	3.833	18%
NY	17.899	64	3.576	17%
CA	21.820	78	3.575	18%
MD	4.419	15.5	3.508	13%
IL	11.265	38	3.373	15%
PA	11.834	38	3.211	17%
GA	5.026	16	3.183	13%
LA	3.924	12	3.058	13%
VA	5.347	15.5	2.899	15%
AR	2.104	6	2.852	18%
OH	10.727	28	2.610	15%
NJ	7.268	18	2.477	13%
CO	2.550	5	1.961	16%
CT	3.070	6	1.955	15%
TN	4.259	8	1.879	10%
WA	4.562	7	1.856	11%
AZ	2.247	4	1.781	17%
SC	2.855	5	1.751	20%
WI	1.847	7	1.534	12%
IA	2.870	4	1.394	17%
KS	2.306	3	1.301	9%
OR	2.362	3	1.270	10%
MA	5.713	7	1.225	13%
FL	8.265	10	1.210	9%
OK	2.793	3	1.074	7%
MO	4.798	5	1.042	8%
MN	3.942	4	1.015	8%
TX	12.714	12	0.944	6%
UT	4.999	1	0.794	5%
NE	1.528	1	0.655	9%
ME	1.060			
NM	1.158			
VT	3.772			
DC	0.698	11	15.771	23%
RI	0.949	3	3.161	30%
NV	0.644	2	3.106	14%
WV	0.402	3	1.624	13%
ND	0.636	1	1.572	33%
MT	0.741	1	1.350	17%
ID	0.829	1	1.206	25%
AK	0.352			
DE	0.572			
HI	0.878			
NH	0.830			
SD	0.678			
WY	0.402			
XX		3		1%
TOT	218.58	570	2.608	14%

1980-1989

State	Pop (M)	#	Con	%
MD	4.810	23.5	4.886	20%
AL	3.966	18	4.539	28%
VA	6.078	27.5	4.525	26%
CT	3.197	14	4.379	34%
AR	2.318	10	4.314	29%
GA	5.971	25	4.187	20%
LA	4.212	17	4.037	19%
NC	6.252	25	3.999	21%
MS	2.547	10	3.927	15%
IL	11.681	44	3.767	17%
KY	3.673	13	3.539	13%
KS	2.421	8	3.305	24%
IN	5.518	18	3.262	10%
NY	17.774	57	3.207	15%
NE	1.574	5	3.177	45%
CA	26.715	83	3.107	19%
MI	9.255	27	2.917	16%
NJ	7.547	21	2.783	15%
TN	4.734	13	2.746	16%
OH	10.822	29	2.680	16%
WA	4.799	12	2.668	18%
OK	3.086	8	2.592	18%
FL	11.339	27	2.381	25%
OR	2.737	6	2.192	21%
AZ	3.202	7	2.186	29%
UT	5.767	3	1.884	14%
PA	11.875	20	1.684	9%
TX	15.608	26	1.666	14%
CO	3.092	5	1.617	16%
SC	3.303	5	1.514	20%
MN	4.226	6	1.420	12%
MO	5.017	7	1.395	12%
MA	5.877	8	1.361	15%
WI	1.872	6	1.250	11%
NV	1.001	1	1.000	7%
NM	1.407	1	0.711	13%
IA	2.846	1	0.351	4%
HI	1.047			
ME	1.177			
NH	1.015			
VT	4.499			
DC	0.623	11	17.671	23%
ID	0.976	2	2.049	50%
DE	0.631	1	1.585	20%
MT	0.793	1	1.261	17%
RI	0.976	1	1.025	10%
WV	0.463	1	0.534	4%
AK	0.475			
ND	0.647			
SD	0.693			
WY	0.463			
XX		19		6%
TOT	241.408	662	2.742	17%

1990-1999

State	Pop (M)	#	Con	%
MS	2.763	18	6.516	26%
MD	5.542	23	4.150	19%
LA	4.356	18	4.132	20%
GA	8.154	30	3.679	25%
TN	5.587	20	3.580	25%
MI	9.610	33	3.434	19%
NJ	8.219	25	3.042	18%
AL	4.375	13	2.971	20%
OK	3.417	10	2.927	22%
IL	12.427	35	2.817	14%
IA	2.893	8	2.766	33%
KY	4.000	11	2.750	11%
VA	7.337	20	2.726	19%
AR	2.620	7	2.672	21%
IN	5.984	15	2.507	9%
CT	3.403	8	2.351	20%
CA	33.361	78	2.338	18%
NC	8.005	18	2.249	15%
SC	4.024	9	2.237	36%
OH	11.195	25	2.233	14%
PA	12.244	25	2.042	11%
KS	2.649	5	1.888	15%
NE	1.688	3	1.778	27%
NY	18.766	33	1.759	9%
WI	1.807	9	1.707	16%
MN	4.821	8	1.660	16%
NH	1.217	2	1.643	25%
MO	5.553	9	1.621	15%
MA	6.305	10	1.586	18%
NV	1.923	3	1.560	21%
TX	20.885	32	1.532	17%
CO	4.160	6	1.442	19%
FL	15.738	22	1.398	20%
WA	5.274	8	1.388	12%
UT	7.035	3	1.331	14%
NM	1.763	2	1.135	25%
OR	3.334	3	0.900	10%
ID	1.277	1	0.783	25%
AZ	5.141	2	0.389	8%
HI	1.202			
ME	1.273			
RI	1.028			
VT	5.766			
DC	0.604	6	9.942	13%
DE	0.776	3	3.868	60%
AK	0.624	1	1.603	33%
ND	0.643	1	1.555	33%
SD	0.754	1	1.326	25%
WV	0.499	2	1.107	9%
MT	0.887			
WY	0.499			
XX		51		16%
TOT	278.25	669	2.404	16%

2000-2009

State	Pop (M)	#	Con	%
MD	6.037	27.5	4.555	23%
MS	2.960	12	4.055	18%
LA	4.513	17	3.767	19%
WA	5.671	21	3.137	32%
IL	12.870	37	2.875	14%
MI	9.927	27	2.720	16%
WI	1.836	14	2.469	25%
NJ	8.750	21	2.400	15%
OR	3.829	9	2.351	31%
NC	9.458	22	2.326	18%
IN	6.453	14	2.169	8%
GA	9.758	21	2.152	17%
PA	12.654	24	1.897	11%
CA	37.108	67	1.806	15%
TX	24.964	45	1.803	24%
KS	2.836	5	1.763	15%
TN	6.321	11	1.740	14%
AL	4.744	8	1.686	12%
OH	11.540	19	1.646	10%
OK	3.719	6	1.613	13%
NY	19.46	31.0	1.593	8%
NH	1.321	2	1.514	25%
UT	7.942	4	1.442	19%
CT	3.546	5	1.410	12%
FL	18.670	25	1.339	23%
MO	5.988	8	1.336	13%
MA	6.571	8	1.218	15%
MN	5.285	6	1.135	12%
AR	2.902	3	1.034	9%
CO	5.027	5	0.995	16%
IA	3.027	3	0.991	13%
RI	1.053	1	0.950	10%
KY	4.327	4	0.924	4%
VA	8.242	6.5	0.789	6%
NV	2.672	2	0.749	14%
AZ	6.494	3	0.462	13%
SC	4.593	2	0.435	8%
HI	1.328			
ID	1.557			
ME	1.323			
NE	1.812			
NM	2.035			
VT	6.694			
DC	0.601	7	11.650	15%
AK	0.704	2	2.840	67%
SD	0.813	2	2.460	50%
WY	0.554	1	1.806	13%
WV	0.554	2	1.089	9%
DE	0.891			
MT	0.982			
ND	0.660			
XX		132		42%
TOT	312	685	2.195	16%

2010-2016

State	Pop (M)	#	Con	Con
IN	6.484	19	2.930	11%
MD	6.074	16	2.634	14%
VA	8.302	21	2.530	20%
GA	9.688	24	2.477	20%
NV	2.701	6	2.222	43%
LA	4.533	9	1.985	10%
TN	6.346	12	1.891	15%
NJ	8.792	16	1.820	12%
IL	12.831	22	1.715	9%
NC	9.535	16	1.678	13%
TX	25.146	41	1.631	22%
WI	1.853	9	1.583	16%
CA	37.254	57	1.530	13%
NH	1.316	2	1.519	25%
MI	9.884	14	1.416	8%
MA	6.548	9	1.375	16%
AR	2.9159	4	1.372	12%
MS	2.967	4	1.348	6%
OK	3.751	5	1.333	11%
MN	5.304	7	1.320	14%
PA	12.702	16	1.260	7%
AL	4.780	6	1.255	9%
NY	19.378	24	1.239	6%
OH	11.537	14	1.214	8%
WA	5.687	8	1.190	12%
MO	5.989	7	1.169	12%
CT	3.574	4	1.119	10%
UT	8.001	3	1.085	14%
KS	2.853	3	1.051	9%
OR	3.831	4	1.044	14%
NM	2.059	2	0.971	25%
FL	18.801	18	0.957	16%
RI	1.053	1	0.950	10%
AZ	6.392	5	0.782	21%
KY	4.339	3	0.691	3%
IA	3.046	2	0.657	8%
SC	4.625	3	0.649	12%
CO	5.029	2	0.398	6%
HI	1.360			0%
ID	1.568			0%
ME	1.328			
NE	1.826			
VT	6.725			
DC	0.602	2	3.324	4%
DE	0.898	1	1.114	20%
MT	0.989	1	1.011	17%
WV	0.564	1	0.540	4%
AK	0.710			
ND	0.673			
SD	0.814			
WY	0.564			
XX		103		33%
TOT	313.16	544	1.737	13%

SO-2: Concentration of NBA Players by Games Played

100+ GP					200+ GP					300+ GP					400+ GP					500+ GP				
State	Pop (M)	# Players	Con	%	State	Pop (M)	# Players	Con	%	State	Pop (M)	# Players	Con	%	State	Pop (M)	# Players	Con	%	State	Pop (M)	# Players	Con	%
IN	5.149	95	18.449	55%	LA	3.679	49	13.320	54%	LA	3.679	39	10.602	43%	LA	3.679	35	9.515	38%	IN	5.149	39	7.574	23%
MS	2.470	44	17.812	65%	IN	5.149	68	13.206	40%	MD	4.303	43	9.992	36%	MD	4.303	38.5	8.946	33%	LA	3.679	27	7.340	30%
LA	3.679	60	16.311	66%	MD	4.303	54	12.548	46%	IN	5.149	51	9.904	30%	IN	5.149	45	8.739	26%	MS	2.470	17	6.882	25%
MD	4.303	69.5	16.150	59%	MS	2.470	30	12.144	44%	NC	6.087	55	9.035	46%	MS	2.470	20	8.096	29%	MD	4.303	29.5	6.855	25%
KY	3.509	54	15.390	55%	KY	3.509	37	10.545	38%	MS	2.470	22	8.906	32%	NC	6.087	48	7.885	40%	NC	6.087	41	6.735	34%
IL	10.867	143	13.159	56%	NC	6.087	63	10.349	53%	IL	10.867	92	8.466	36%	GA	5.821	42	7.215	34%	KY	3.509	21	5.985	21%
GA	5.821	76	13.055	62%	IL	10.867	112	10.307	44%	GA	5.821	49	8.417	40%	IL	10.867	75	6.902	29%	AR	2.251	13	5.776	38%
NC	6.087	79	12.978	66%	GA	5.821	59	10.135	48%	KY	3.509	28	7.980	29%	KY	3.509	24	6.840	24%	GA	5.821	32	5.497	26%
CA	22.620	267	11.804	60%	CA	22.620	216	9.549	49%	CA	22.620	173	7.648	39%	CA	22.620	153	6.764	35%	IL	10.867	58	5.337	23%
NJ	6.860	77	11.224	55%	NJ	6.860	60	8.746	43%	AL	3.754	28	7.459	43%	VA	5.588	33.5	5.995	32%	CA	22.620	120	5.305	27%
OH	9.997	109	10.903	59%	MI	8.346	70	8.387	41%	VA	5.588	39	6.979	37%	AL	3.754	22	5.861	34%	VA	5.588	28.5	5.100	27%
MI	8.346	91	10.903	54%	NY	17.230	143	8.299	38%	NJ	6.860	47	6.851	34%	AR	2.251	13	5.776	38%	NY	17.230	81	4.701	22%
NY	17.230	186	10.795	50%	OH	9.997	82	8.203	44%	PA	11.575	78	6.739	35%	PA	11.575	65	5.616	29%	MI	8.346	37	4.433	22%
WA	4.098	44	10.738	68%	VA	5.588	45	8.052	43%	NY	17.230	115	6.674	31%	NY	17.230	95	5.514	25%	WA	4.098	18	4.393	28%
VA	5.588	59.5	10.647	57%	AL	3.754	30	7.992	46%	OH	9.997	64	6.402	35%	NJ	6.860	37	5.393	27%	OH	9.997	43	4.301	23%
AL	3.754	39	10.389	60%	NV	1.049	8	7.625	57%	MI	8.346	53	6.350	31%	MI	8.346	45	5.392	26%	PA	11.575	48	4.147	22%
AR	2.251	23	10.218	68%	PA	11.575	88	7.603	39%	AR	2.251	14	6.220	41%	WV	1.873	10	5.339	43%	NJ	6.860	27	3.936	19%
PA	11.575	115	9.935	52%	CT	2.848	21	7.374	51%	WA	4.098	25	6.101	38%	WA	4.098	20	4.881	31%	SC	3.099	12	3.872	48%
CT	2.848	26	9.130	63%	AR	2.251	16	7.108	47%	NV	1.049	6	5.719	43%	KS	2.332	11	4.717	32%	CT	2.848	11	3.863	27%
OK	2.879	24	8.336	53%	WA	4.098	29	7.077	45%	OR	2.452	14	5.709	48%	OH	9.997	46	4.601	25%	KS	2.332	9	3.859	26%
TN	4.479	37	8.261	47%	MO	4.844	30	6.193	50%	CT	2.848	16	5.618	39%	CT	2.848	13	4.565	32%	AL	3.754	14	3.730	22%
OR	2.452	19	7.748	66%	OR	2.452	15	6.117	52%	WV	1.873	10	5.339	43%	TN	4.479	19	4.242	24%	OR	2.452	9	3.670	31%
KS	2.332	18	7.719	53%	KS	2.332	14	6.003	41%	KS	2.332	12	5.146	35%	CO	2.833	12	4.235	38%	FL	9.560	35	3.661	32%
NV	1.049	8	7.625	57%	OK	2.879	17	5.905	38%	MO	4.844	24	4.955	40%	SC	3.099	13	4.195	52%	WV	1.873	6	3.203	26%
MO	4.844	34	7.019	57%	WV	1.873	11	5.873	48%	OK	2.879	14	4.863	31%	OK	2.879	12	4.168	27%	IA	2.811	9	3.201	38%
TX	14.515	101	6.958	54%	FL	9.560	54	5.649	49%	TN	4.479	21	4.689	27%	OR	2.452	10	4.078	34%	TN	4.479	14	3.126	18%
WV	1.873	13	6.940	57%	TN	4.479	25	5.582	32%	FL	9.560	44	4.603	40%	FL	9.560	37	3.870	34%	WI	4.489	14	3.119	25%
CO	2.833	19	6.706	59%	MN	4.005	20	4.994	40%	CO	2.833	13	4.588	41%	NV	1.049	4	3.812	29%	TX	14.515	43	2.962	23%
FL	9.560	64	6.695	58%	CO	2.833	14	4.941	44%	SC	3.099	14	4.517	56%	WI	4.489	17	3.787	30%	NV	1.049	3	2.859	21%
MN	4.005	26	6.492	52%	TX	14.515	71	4.891	38%	TX	14.515	58	3.996	31%	MO	4.844	18	3.716	30%	CO	2.833	8	2.824	25%
UT	1.492	9	6.033	43%	SC	3.099	15	4.840	60%	WI	4.489	17	3.787	30%	TX	14.515	52	3.582	28%	AZ	2.967	8	2.696	33%
WI	4.489	25	5.570	44%	UT	1.492	33	4.693	157%	MN	4.005	15	3.745	30%	IA	2.811	9	3.201	38%	MO	4.844	13	2.684	22%
MA	5.595	29	5.183	53%	WI	4.489	20	4.456	35%	IA	2.811	10	3.557	42%	AZ	2.967	8	2.696	33%	UT	1.492	3	2.011	14%
SC	3.099	16	5.162	64%	IA	2.811	12	4.268	50%	AZ	2.967	10	3.370	42%	MN	4.005	10	2.497	20%	NE	1.539	3	1.950	27%
IA	2.811	14	4.980	58%	AZ	2.967	12	4.044	50%	UT	1.492	4	2.681	19%	UT	1.492	3	2.011	14%	NM	1.260	2	1.588	25%
AZ	2.967	13	4.381	54%	MA	5.595	17	3.039	31%	MA	5.595	14	2.502	25%	NE	1.539	3	1.950	27%	MA	5.595	8	1.430	15%
NE	1.539	5	3.249	45%	NM	1.260	3	2.382	38%	NM	1.260	3	2.382	38%	MA	5.595	10	1.787	18%	OK	2.879	4	1.389	9%
NM	1.260	4	3.175	50%	NE	1.539	3	1.950	27%	NE	1.539	3	1.950	27%	NM	1.260	2	1.588	25%	ME	1.091			
ME	1.091				ME	1.091				ME	1.091				ME									
DC	0.680	29	42.626	60%	DC	0.680	24	35.276	50%	DC	0.680	18	26.457	38%	DC	0.680	15	22.048	31%	DC	0.680	11	16.168	23%
WY	0.405	4	9.878	50%	AK	0.396	2	5.055	67%	AK	0.396	2	5.055	67%	AK	0.396	2	5.055	67%	AK	0.396	2	5.055	67%
AK	0.396	3	7.582	100%	WY	0.405	2	4.939	25%	SD	0.707	2	2.829	50%	SD	0.707	2	2.829	50%	SD	0.707	2	2.829	50%
RI	0.919	6	6.526	60%	RI	0.919	4	4.350	40%	WY	0.405	1	2.469	13%	WY	0.405	1	2.469	13%	ND	0.640	1	1.562	33%
DE	0.579	3	5.184	60%	SD	0.707	2	2.829	50%	NH	0.880	2	2.272	25%	NH	0.880	2	2.272	25%	NH	0.880	1	1.136	13%
NH	0.880	4	4.545	50%	MT	0.760	2	2.632	33%	ND	0.640	1	1.562	33%	ND	0.640	1	1.562	33%	HI	0.893	1	1.120	100%
ND	0.640	2	3.123	67%	NH	0.880	2	2.272	25%	MT	0.760	1	1.316	17%	MT	0.760	1	1.316	17%	DE	0.579			
SD	0.707	2	2.829	50%	ND	0.640	1	1.562	33%	HI	0.893	1	1.120	100%	HI	0.893	1	1.120	100%	ID	0.946			
MT	0.760	2	2.632	33%	HI	0.893	1	1.120	100%	RI	0.919	1	1.088	10%	DE	0.579				MT	0.760			
HI	0.893	1	1.120	100%	ID	0.946	1	1.057	25%	DE	0.579				ID	0.946				RI	0.919			
ID	0.946	1	1.057	25%	DE	0.579				ID	0.946				RI	0.919				VT	0.487			
VT	0.487				VT	0.487				VT	0.487				VT	0.487				WY	0.405			
XX		163		52%	XX		120		38%	XX		88		28%	XX		70		22%	XX		50		16%
TOT		2276		56%	TOT		1768		44%	TOT		1436		35%	TOT		1210		30%	TOT		972		24%

SO-2: Concentration of NBA Players by Games Played by State

600+ GP

State	Pop (M)	# Player	Con	%
MS	2.470	14	5.667	21%
IN	5.149	26	5.049	15%
NC	6.087	30	4.928	25%
LA	3.679	18	4.893	20%
AR	2.251	11	4.887	32%
KY	3.509	17	4.845	17%
IL	10.867	49	4.509	19%
GA	5.821	26	4.466	21%
MD	4.303	19	4.415	16%
VA	5.588	24	4.295	23%
MI	8.346	32	3.834	19%
CA	22.620	85	3.758	19%
NY	17.230	63	3.656	17%
SC	3.099	11	3.549	44%
PA	11.575	40	3.456	18%
NJ	6.860	23	3.353	17%
OH	9.997	33	3.301	18%
WA	4.098	13	3.173	20%
CT	2.848	9	3.160	22%
FL	9.560	29	3.034	26%
KS	2.332	7	3.002	21%
AL	3.754	11	2.930	17%
NV	1.049	3	2.859	21%
OR	2.452	7	2.855	24%
TX	14.515	37	2.549	20%
TN	4.479	10	2.233	13%
WI	4.489	10	2.228	18%
WV	1.873	4	2.135	17%
AZ	2.967	6	2.022	25%
MO	4.844	9	1.858	15%
NM	1.260	2	1.588	25%
MN	4.005	6	1.498	12%
IA	2.811	4	1.423	17%
CO	2.833	4	1.412	13%
OK	2.879	4	1.389	9%
UT	1.492	2	1.341	10%
MA	5.595	5	0.894	9%
NE	1.539	1	0.650	9%
ME	1.091			
DC	0.680	6	8.819	13%
SD	0.707	2	2.829	50%
AK	0.396	1	2.527	33%
ND	0.640	1	1.562	33%
NH	0.880	1	1.136	13%
DE	0.579			
HI	0.893			
ID	0.946			
MT	0.760			
RI	0.919			
VT	0.487			
WY	0.405			
XX		39		12%
TOT		748		18%

700+ GP

State	Pop (M)	# Player	Con	%
MS	2.470	14	5.667	21%
LA	3.679	15	4.078	16%
AR	2.251	9	3.998	26%
NC	6.087	24	3.943	20%
GA	5.821	21	3.607	17%
IL	10.867	38	3.497	15%
MI	8.346	28	3.355	16%
SC	3.099	10	3.227	40%
IN	5.149	16	3.107	9%
VA	5.588	17	3.042	16%
OR	2.452	7	2.855	24%
MD	4.303	12	2.788	10%
CA	22.620	63	2.785	14%
NY	17.230	47	2.728	13%
AL	3.754	10	2.664	15%
CT	2.848	7	2.458	17%
PA	11.575	28	2.419	13%
OH	9.997	24	2.401	13%
KY	3.509	8	2.280	8%
WA	4.098	9	2.196	14%
NJ	6.860	15	2.186	11%
KS	2.332	5	2.144	15%
WV	1.873	4	2.135	17%
WI	4.489	9	2.005	16%
FL	9.560	19	1.988	17%
TX	14.515	26	1.791	14%
TN	4.479	8	1.786	10%
AZ	2.967	5	1.685	21%
CO	2.833	4	1.412	13%
OK	2.879	4	1.389	10%
UT	1.492	2	1.341	10%
MO	4.844	6	1.239	10%
IA	2.811	3	1.067	13%
NV	1.049	1	0.953	7%
MA	5.595	5	0.894	9%
NM	1.260	1	0.794	13%
MN	4.005	3	0.749	6%
NE	1.539	1	0.650	9%
ME	1.091			
DC	0.680	4	5.879	8%
SD	0.707	2	2.829	50%
AK	0.396	1	2.527	33%
ND	0.640	1	1.562	33%
NH	0.880	1	1.136	13%
DE	0.579			
HI	0.893			
ID	0.946			
MT	0.760			
RI	0.919			
VT	0.487			
WY	0.405			
XX		25		8%
TOT		558		14%

800+ GP

State	Pop (M)	# Player	Con	%
MS	2.470	11	4.453	16%
NC	6.087	19	3.121	16%
LA	3.679	11	2.990	12%
AR	2.251	6	2.666	18%
SC	3.099	8	2.581	32%
VA	5.588	14	2.505	13%
IL	10.867	26	2.393	10%
GA	5.821	13	2.233	11%
WA	4.098	9	2.196	14%
IN	5.149	11	2.136	6%
AL	3.754	8	2.131	12%
CA	22.620	42	1.857	10%
NY	17.230	31	1.799	8%
WI	4.489	8	1.782	14%
CT	2.848	5	1.756	12%
MI	8.346	14	1.677	8%
OR	2.452	4	1.631	14%
MD	4.303	7	1.627	6%
WV	1.873	3	1.602	13%
OH	9.997	16	1.601	9%
PA	11.575	17	1.469	8%
UT	1.492	2	1.341	10%
KS	2.332	3	1.286	9%
FL	9.560	11	1.151	10%
TX	14.515	16	1.102	9%
CO	2.833	3	1.059	9%
OK	2.879	3	1.042	7%
NJ	6.860	6	0.875	4%
KY	3.509	3	0.855	3%
MO	4.844	4	0.826	7%
NM	1.260	1	0.794	13%
MN	4.005	3	0.749	6%
IA	2.811	2	0.711	8%
AZ	2.967	2	0.674	8%
TN	4.479	3	0.670	4%
NE	1.539	1	0.650	9%
MA	5.595	3	0.536	5%
ME	1.091			
NV	1.049			
DC	0.680	2	2.940	4%
AK	0.396	1	2.527	33%
ND	0.640	1	1.562	33%
SD	0.707	1	1.415	25%
DE	0.579			
HI	0.893			
ID	0.946			
MT	0.760			
NH	0.880			
RI	0.919			
VT	0.487			
WY	0.405			
XX		20		6%
TOT		372		9%

900+ GP

State	Pop (M)	# Player	Con	%
MS	2.470	7	2.834	10%
AR	2.251	5	2.221	15%
SC	3.099	6	1.936	24%
LA	3.679	7	1.903	8%
NC	6.087	11	1.807	9%
CT	2.848	5	1.756	12%
GA	5.821	10	1.718	8%
VA	5.588	9.5	1.700	9%
IL	10.867	18	1.656	7%
AL	3.754	6	1.598	9%
WA	4.098	6	1.464	9%
IN	5.149	7	1.359	4%
MD	4.303	5.5	1.278	5%
OR	2.452	3	1.223	10%
MI	8.346	9	1.078	5%
WV	1.873	2	1.068	9%
CO	2.833	3	1.059	9%
NY	17.230	18	1.045	5%
CA	22.620	23	1.017	5%
OH	9.997	9	0.900	5%
WI	4.489	4	0.891	7%
NM	1.260	1	0.794	13%
FL	9.560	7	0.732	6%
PA	11.575	8	0.691	4%
TX	14.515	10	0.689	5%
AZ	2.967	2	0.674	8%
TN	4.479	2	0.447	3%
KS	2.332	1	0.429	3%
OK	2.879	1	0.347	5%
KY	3.509	1	0.285	1%
MN	4.005	1	0.250	2%
MO	4.844	1	0.206	2%
MA	5.595	1	0.179	2%
NJ	6.860	1	0.146	1%
IA	2.811			
ME	1.091			
NE	1.539			
NV	1.049			
UT	1.492			
DC	0.680	1	1.470	2%
SD	0.707	1	1.415	25%
AK	0.396			
DE	0.579			
HI	0.893			
ID	0.946			
MT	0.760			
ND	0.640			
NH	0.880			
RI	0.919			
VT	0.487			
WY	0.405			
XX		12		4%
TOT		224		5%

1000+ GP

State	Pop (M)	# Player	Con	%
AR	2.251	5	2.221	15%
LA	3.679	6	1.631	7%
WA	4.098	6	1.464	9%
SC	3.099	4	1.291	16%
VA	5.588	7	1.253	7%
NC	6.087	6	0.986	5%
IL	10.867	9	0.828	4%
OR	2.452	2	0.816	7%
MS	2.470	2	0.810	3%
AL	3.754	3	0.799	5%
CO	2.833	2	0.706	6%
CT	2.848	2	0.702	5%
GA	5.821	4	0.687	3%
AZ	2.967	2	0.674	8%
CA	22.620	15	0.663	3%
OH	9.997	6	0.600	3%
IN	5.149	3	0.583	2%
NY	17.230	10	0.580	3%
WV	1.873	1	0.534	4%
MI	8.346	4	0.479	2%
FL	9.560	3	0.314	3%
TX	14.515	4	0.276	2%
PA	11.575	3	0.259	1%
TN	4.479	1	0.223	1%
WI	4.489	1	0.223	2%
MA	5.595	1	0.179	2%
IA	2.811			
KS	2.332			
KY	3.509			
MD	4.303			
ME	1.091			
MN	4.005			
MO	4.844			
NE	1.539			
NJ	6.860			
NM	1.260			
NV	1.049			
OK	2.879			
UT	1.492			
SD	0.707	1	1.415	25%
AK	0.396			
DC	0.680			
DE	0.579			
HI	0.893			
ID	0.946			
MT	0.760			
ND	0.640			
NH	0.880			
RI	0.919			
VT	0.487			
WY	0.405			
XX		9		3%
TOT		121		3%

SO-3: Concentration of ABA Players

State	Pop (M)	# Players	Con	# NBA Players	% NBA Players
KY	3.441	30	8.718	9	30.00%
IN	5.343	37	6.925	14	37.84%
MS	2.369	12	5.066	4	33.33%
PA	11.834	52	4.394	19	36.54%
NC	5.479	23	4.198	9	39.13%
UT	1.260	5	3.968		
LA	3.924	15	3.823	8	53.33%
TN	4.259	16	3.757	6	37.50%
MD	4.419	15.5	3.508	8.5	54.84%
AR	2.104	7	3.327	2	28.57%
NY	17.899	53	2.961	23	43.40%
WV	1.847	5	2.707	2	40.00%
MT	0.741	2	2.701		
NJ	7.268	19	2.614	7	36.84%
MI	9.071	23	2.536	12	52.17%
IL	11.265	27	2.397	10	37.04%
VA	5.347	12.5	2.338	4.5	36.00%
AL	3.668	8	2.181	5	62.50%
KS	2.306	5	2.168	1	20.00%
OH	10.727	23	2.144	13	56.52%
RI	0.949	2	2.107	1	50.00%
CA	21.820	44	2.016	20	45.45%
GA	5.026	10	1.990	2	20.00%
WA	3.772	7	1.856	4	57.14%
OK	2.793	5	1.791	1	20.00%
NM	1.158	2	1.727		
MO	4.798	8	1.668	2	25.00%
TX	12.714	19	1.494	5	26.32%
NE	1.528	2	1.309		
OR	2.362	3	1.270	2	66.67%
ID	0.829	1	1.206		
CT	3.070	3	0.977	2	66.67%
FL	8.265	7	0.847		
CO	2.550	2	0.784	1	50.00%
MN	3.942	3	0.761	1	33.33%
AZ	2.247	1	0.445		
WI	4.562	2	0.438	1	50.00%
SC	2.855	1	0.350	1	100.00%
MA	5.713	1	0.175	1	100.00%
DC	0.698	9	12.903	5	55.56%
WY	0.402	1	2.491		
NV	0.644	1	1.553		
XX		2			
Total		**517**		**206**	**39.85%**

SO-4: Concentration of NCAA All-Americans by Decade

All Years — Number of Selections				All Years — Number of Players Selected				1905-1939 — Number of Selections					1905-1939 — Number of Players Selected					1940-1959 — Number of Selections					1940-1959 — Number of Players Selected				
State	Pop(M)	#	Con	State	Pop(M)	#	Con	State	Pop(M)	#	Con	%	State	Pop(M)	#	Con	%	State	Pop(M)	#	Con	%	State	Pop(M)	#	Con	%
IN	4.045	109	26.949	IN	4.045	72	17.801	IN	2.963	27	9.113	24.8%	IN	2.963	19	6.413	26.4%	IN	4.019	25	6.220	22.9%	KS	1.965	8	3.653	33.3%
KS	1.959	35	17.866	KS	1.959	24	12.251	KS	1.723	14	8.128	40.0%	KS	1.723	9	5.225	37.5%	KS	1.965	12	6.108	34.3%	IN	4.019	16	3.462	22.2%
UT	1.042	15	14.400	OR	1.726	21	12.165	WI	2.622	14	5.339	58.3%	WI	2.622	12	4.576	54.5%	KY	2.950	14	4.746	42.4%	WV	1.942	5	2.577	62.5%
MD	3.135	42	13.396	MD	3.135	36.5	11.641	IL	6.495	31	4.773	27.9%	WA	1.263	5	3.958	31.3%	WV	1.942	8	4.120	61.5%	KY	2.950	8	2.366	33.3%
NC	4.502	60	13.327	IL	8.578	85	9.909	WA	1.263	5	3.958	29.4%	IL	6.495	20	3.079	23.5%	IL	8.907	30	3.368	27.0%	OK	2.287	6	2.174	31.6%
IL	8.578	111	12.940	UT	1.042	10	9.600	MO	3.444	11	3.194	28.9%	NJ	3.156	7	2.218	19.4%	OK	2.287	6	2.623	25.0%	IL	8.907	21	2.140	24.7%
OR	1.726	21	12.165	NC	4.502	38	8.440	NY	10.567	32	3.028	22.2%	NY	10.567	22	2.082	21.0%	OH	8.198	20	2.440	31.3%	PA	10.580	17	1.541	27.4%
KY	2.888	33	11.428	KY	2.888	24	8.311	NJ	3.156	8	2.535	18.6%	MO	3.444	7	2.033	28.0%	PA	10.580	25	2.363	27.2%	OH	8.198	13	1.478	28.3%
NY	13.631	144	10.564	OK	2.300	19	8.260	IA	2.374	6	2.528	30.0%	MN	2.314	4	1.729	33.3%	MN	3.071	7	2.279	43.8%	IA	2.640	4	1.462	26.7%
OK	2.300	24	10.434	NY	13.631	105	7.703	PA	8.444	21	2.487	22.8%	IA	2.374	4	1.685	26.7%	WA	2.327	5	2.148	29.4%	WA	2.327	4	1.106	25.0%
PA	9.609	92	9.574	NJ	5.116	36	7.037	CA	3.975	9	2.264	8.8%	OK	1.842	3	1.629	15.8%	CO	1.406	3	2.134	33.3%	MO	4.021	5	1.093	20.0%
MO	4.014	38	9.466	AR	1.885	13	6.898	MN	2.314	4	1.729	25.0%	CA	3.975	6	1.509	7.3%	MO	4.021	8	1.990	21.1%	MN	3.071	4	1.082	
VA	4.163	38	9.128	PA	9.609	62	6.452	OK	1.842	3	1.629	12.5%	WV	1.467	2	1.363	7.7%	NY	15.045	25	1.662	17.4%	NY	15.045	17	1.069	16.2%
NJ	5.116	43	8.406	VA	4.163	26.5	6.365	KY	2.463	4	1.624	12.1%	KY	2.463	3	1.218	12.5%	CA	11.115	18	1.619	17.6%	WI	3.517	4	0.978	18.2%
WV	1.566	13	8.301	MI	6.193	39	6.297	WV	1.467	2	1.363	15.4%	AR	1.688	2	1.185	15.4%	TN	3.264	5	1.532	18.5%	TN	3.264	4	0.955	20.0%
OH	7.793	64	8.213	WI	3.529	22	6.233	AR	1.688	2	1.185	13.3%	PA	8.444	10	1.184	16.1%	IA	2.640	4	1.515	20.0%	NJ	5.040	5	0.842	13.9%
IA	2.448	20	8.171	MO	4.014	25	6.228	NE	3.396	4	1.178	57.1%	MA	3.718	4	1.076	30.8%	NE	1.351	2	1.480	28.6%	CA	11.115	15	0.822	18.3%
MI	6.193	50	8.073	IA	2.448	15	6.128	NC	2.680	3	1.119	5.0%	MD	1.697	1.5	0.884	4.1%	NJ	5.040	7	1.389	16.3%	CO	1.406	2	0.801	33.3%
AR	1.885	15	7.959	OH	7.793	46	5.903	MA	3.718	4	1.076	20.0%	NE	3.396	3	0.883	60.0%	NC	4.065	5	1.230	8.3%	NE	1.351	1	0.672	20.0%
TN	3.461	27	7.802	TN	3.461	20	5.779	MI	3.800	4	1.053	8.0%	MI	3.800	3	0.790	7.7%	WI	3.517	4	1.137	16.7%	NC	4.065	3	0.524	7.9%
LA	2.797	21	7.507	WA	2.874	16	5.567	VA	2.485	2.5	1.006	6.6%	NC	2.680	2	0.746	5.3%	LA	2.778	3	1.080	14.3%	OR	1.465	1	0.465	4.8%
CA	14.917	102	6.838	CA	14.917	82	5.497	OH	5.648	5	0.885	7.8%	CT	1.344	1	0.744	10.0%	MA	4.725	5	1.058	25.0%	TX	7.927	6	0.458	14.3%
WI	3.529	24	6.800	LA	2.797	15	5.362	MD	1.697	1.5	0.884	3.6%	OH	5.648	4	0.708	8.7%	TX	7.927	8	1.009	17.0%	AR	1.881	1	0.443	7.7%
CT	2.138	14	6.548	WV	1.566	8	5.109	CT	1.344	1	0.744	7.1%	TX	4.770	3	0.629	7.1%	CT	2.088	2	0.958	14.3%	CT	2.088	1	0.412	10.0%
WA	2.874	17	5.915	CT	2.138	10	4.677	TX	4.770	3	0.629	6.4%	VA	2.485	1.5	0.604	5.7%	GA	3.508	3	0.855	15.0%	MS	2.178	1	0.410	14.3%
MN	3.140	16	5.096	GA	4.400	18	4.091	AL	2.359				AL	2.359				VA	3.679	3	0.815	7.9%	VA	3.679	1.5	0.408	5.7%
TX	10.273	47	4.575	TX	10.273	42	4.088	FL	1.123				FL	1.123				OR	1.465	1	0.683	4.8%	MA	4.725	2	0.386	15.4%
GA	4.400	20	4.545	MN	3.140	12	3.822	GA	2.751				GA	2.751				AR	1.881	1	0.532	6.7%	GA	3.508	2	0.369	11.1%
CO	1.998	9	4.503	MS	2.070	7	3.382	LA	1.860				LA	1.860				MS	2.178	1	0.459	11.1%	LA	2.778	1	0.313	6.7%
MA	4.541	20	4.404	AL	2.999	10	3.334	MS	1.867				MS	1.867				MD	2.811	1	0.356	2.4%	MD	2.811	0.5	0.178	1.4%
MS	2.070	9	4.348	CO	1.998	6	3.002	SC	1.636				SC	1.636				MI	6.508	1	0.154	2.0%	MI	6.508	1	0.139	2.6%
AL	2.999	13	4.334	MA	4.541	13	2.863	TN	2.415				TN	2.415				AL	3.055				AL	3.055			
NE	2.152	7	3.253	FL	6.169	17	2.756	UT	0.431	8	18.541	53.3%	UT	0.431	6	13.906	60.0%	FL	3.223				FL	3.223			
FL	6.169	20	3.242	NE	2.152	5	2.324	OR	0.783	8	10.221	38.1%	OR	0.783	8	10.221	38.1%	SC	2.137				SC	2.137			
AZ	1.910	6	3.141	AZ	1.910	4	2.094	AZ	0.319	2	6.266	33.3%	ND	0.573	2	3.489	100.0%	WY	0.292	4	13.714	100.0%	WY	0.292	3	8.133	#####
SC	2.390	6	2.510	SC	2.390	5	2.092	ND	0.573	3	5.234	100.0%	AZ	0.319	1	3.133	25.0%	UT	0.714	5	7.003	33.3%	DE	0.346	1	2.019	#####
DC	0.537	18	33.539	DC	0.537	13	24.223	ID	0.378	1	2.647	100.0%	ID	0.378	1	2.647	100.0%	DE	0.346	1	2.893	100.0%	UT	0.714	2	1.496	20.0%
WY	0.300	4	13.340	WY	0.300	3	10.005	DC	0.439	1	2.276	5.6%	DC	0.439	1	2.276	7.7%	DC	0.746	2	2.680	11.1%	DC	0.746	1	1.443	7.7%
AK	0.262	3	11.445	AK	0.262	2	7.630	SD	0.592	1	1.690	100.0%	SD	0.592	1	1.690	100.0%	AK	0.168				AK	0.168			
NV	0.668	4	5.986	NV	0.668	4	5.986	AK	0.076				AK	0.076				AZ	0.858				AZ	0.858			
NH	0.676	4	5.914	NH	0.676	4	5.914	CO	0.887				CO	0.887				HI	0.541				HI	0.541			
ND	0.565	3	5.309	RI	0.740	3	4.055	DE	0.223				DE	0.223				ID	0.596				ID	0.596			
RI	0.740	3	4.055	ND	0.565	2	3.539	HI	0.292				HI	0.292				ME	0.911				ME	0.911			
MT	0.599	2	3.340	MT	0.599	2	3.340	ME	0.770				ME	0.770				MT	0.612				MT	0.612			
DE	0.421	1	2.373	DE	0.421	1	2.373	MT	0.453				MT	0.453				ND	0.631				ND	0.631			
SD	0.613	1	1.631	SD	0.613	1	1.631	NH	0.449				NH	0.449				NH	0.544				NH	0.544			
ID	0.687	1	1.456	ID	0.687	1	1.456	NM	0.368				NM	0.368				NM	0.726				NM	0.726			
HI	0.624			HI	0.624			NV	0.081				NV	0.081				NV	0.187				NV	0.187			
ME	0.902			ME	0.902			RI	0.595				RI	0.595				RI	0.783				RI	0.783			
NM	0.876			NM	0.876			VT	0.354				VT	0.354				SD	0.659				SD	0.659			
VT	0.408			VT	0.408			WY	0.182				WY	0.182				VT	0.376				VT	0.376			
UN		62		UN		55		UN		62		100.0%	UN		55		100.0%	UN					UN				
XX		16		XX		14		XX					XX					XX					XX				
TOT	167.2	1449	8.665	TOT	167.2	1101	6.584	TOT	108.6	306	2.247	16.4%	TOT	108.6	232	2.072	20.5%	TOT	155.4	272	1.757	18.9%	TOT	155.4	186	1.197	17.0%

SO-4: Concentration of NCAA All-Americans by Decade

1960-1969

Number of Selections

State	Pop (M)	#	Con	%
IN	4.936	18	3.647	17%
KY	3.134	7	2.234	21%
WV	1.801	3	1.666	23%
TN	3.750	6	1.600	22%
NC	4.824	7	1.451	12%
LA	3.458	5	1.446	24%
OH	10.198	13	1.275	20%
NY	17.534	21	1.198	15%
MO	4.505	5	1.110	13%
AR	1.856	2	1.078	13%
MI	8.365	9	1.076	18%
MD	3.900	4	1.026	10%
PA	11.572	11	0.951	12%
IL	10.612	8	0.754	7%
NJ	6.635	5	0.754	12%
CT	2.790	2	0.717	14%
FL	5.871	4	0.681	20%
OR	1.933	1	0.517	5%
CA	17.911	9	0.502	9%
KS	2.214	1	0.452	3%
VA	4.694	2	0.426	5%
OK	2.446	1	0.409	4%
AL	3.359	1	0.298	8%
TX	10.408	3	0.288	6%
MA	5.428	1	0.184	5%
AZ	1.547			
CO	1.984			
GA	4.269			
IA	2.793			
MN	3.616			
MS	2.199			
NE	1.450			
SC	2.492			
WA	3.137			
WI	4.191			
DC	0.760	4	5.267	22%
MT	0.686	2	2.915	100%
AK	0.266			
DE	0.499			
HI	0.706			
ID	0.692			
ME	0.984			
ND	0.626			
NH	0.674			
NM	0.988			
NV	0.389			
RI	0.904			
SD	0.674			
UT	0.978			
VT	0.418			
WY	0.332			
UN				
XX				
TOT	192.4	151	0.738	10%

Number of Players Selected

State	Pop (M)	#	Con	%
KY	3.134	6	1.914	25%
IN	4.936	9	1.823	13%
TN	3.750	5	1.334	25%
AR	1.856	2	1.078	15%
MD	3.900	3.5	0.897	10%
OH	10.198	9	0.883	20%
NC	4.824	4	0.829	11%
PA	11.572	9	0.778	15%
MI	8.365	6	0.717	15%
NY	17.534	12	0.684	11%
NJ	6.635	4	0.603	11%
LA	3.458	2	0.578	13%
IL	10.612	6	0.565	7%
WV	1.801	1	0.555	13%
OR	1.933	1	0.517	5%
FL	5.871	3	0.511	18%
KS	2.214	1	0.452	4%
MO	4.505	2	0.444	8%
OK	2.446	1	0.409	5%
CT	2.790	1	0.358	10%
CA	17.911	6	0.335	7%
VA	4.694	1.5	0.320	6%
AL	3.359	1	0.298	10%
TX	10.408	2	0.192	5%
MA	5.428	1	0.184	8%
AZ	1.547			
CO	1.984			
GA	4.269			
IA	2.793			
MN	3.616			
MS	2.199			
NE	1.450			
SC	2.492			
WA	3.137			
WI	4.191			
DC	0.760	3	3.950	23%
MT	0.686	2	2.915	100%
AK	0.266			
DE	0.499			
HI	0.706			
ID	0.692			
ME	0.984			
ND	0.626			
NH	0.674			
NM	0.988			
NV	0.389			
RI	0.904			
SD	0.674			
UT	0.978			
VT	0.418			
WY	0.332			
UN				
XX				
TOT	192.4	101	0.494	9%

1970-1979

Number of Selections

State	Pop (M)	#	Con	%
NC	5.479	18	3.285	30%
AL	3.668	7	1.909	54%
NY	17.899	26	1.453	18%
AR	2.104	3	1.426	20%
IN	5.343	7	1.310	6%
MD	4.419	4.5	1.018	11%
CT	3.070	3	0.977	21%
IL	11.265	10	0.888	9%
CA	21.820	19	0.871	19%
MI	9.071	7	0.772	14%
LA	3.924	3	0.765	14%
OH	10.727	8	0.746	13%
TN	4.259	3	0.704	11%
WI	4.562	3	0.658	13%
PA	11.834	7	0.592	8%
KY	3.441	2	0.581	6%
FL	8.265	4	0.484	20%
OR	2.362	1	0.423	5%
NJ	7.268	3	0.413	7%
CO	2.550	1	0.392	11%
SC	2.855	1	0.350	17%
MA	5.713	2	0.350	10%
VA	5.347	1.5	0.281	4%
MO	4.798	1	0.208	3%
GA	5.026	1	0.199	5%
TX	12.714	1	0.079	2%
AZ	2.247			
IA	2.870			
KS	2.306			
ME	1.060			
MN	3.942			
MS	2.369			
NE	1.528			
NM	1.158			
OK	2.793			
UT	1.260			
WA	3.772			
WV	1.847			
DC	0.698	3	4.301	17%
RI	0.949	2	2.107	67%
NV	0.644	1	1.553	25%
AK	0.352			
DE	0.572			
HI	0.878			
ID	0.829			
MT	0.741			
ND	0.636			
NH	0.830			
SD	0.678			
VT	0.479			
WY	0.402			
UN				
XX				
TOT	214.9	150	0.716	10%

Number of Players Selected

State	Pop (M)	#	Con	%
NC	5.479	9	1.643	24%
NY	17.899	20	1.117	19%
AL	3.668	4	1.091	40%
AR	2.104	2	0.951	15%
IL	11.265	9	0.799	11%
LA	3.924	3	0.765	20%
IN	5.343	4	0.749	6%
MD	4.419	3	0.679	8%
MI	9.071	6	0.661	15%
WI	4.562	3	0.658	14%
CT	3.070	2	0.652	20%
KY	3.441	2	0.581	8%
CA	21.820	12	0.550	15%
TN	4.259	2	0.470	10%
OH	10.727	5	0.466	11%
OR	2.362	1	0.423	5%
PA	11.834	5	0.423	8%
NJ	7.268	3	0.413	8%
CO	2.550	1	0.392	17%
SC	2.855	1	0.350	20%
FL	8.265	2	0.242	12%
MO	4.798	1	0.208	4%
GA	5.026	1	0.199	4%
VA	5.347	1	0.187	4%
MA	5.713	1	0.175	8%
TX	12.714	1	0.079	2%
AZ	2.247			
IA	2.870			
KS	2.306			
ME	1.060			
MN	3.942			
MS	2.369			
NE	1.528			
NM	1.158			
OK	2.793			
UT	1.260			
WA	3.772			
WV	1.847			
DC	0.698	2	2.867	15%
RI	0.949	2	2.107	67%
NV	0.644	1	1.553	25%
AK	0.352			
DE	0.572			
HI	0.878			
ID	0.829			
MT	0.741			
ND	0.636			
NH	0.830			
SD	0.678			
VT	0.479			
WY	0.402			
UN				
XX				
TOT	214.9	107	0.510	9%

1980-1989

Number of Selections

State	Pop (M)	#	Con	%
VA	6.078	12.5	2.057	33%
MS	2.547	5	1.963	56%
OK	3.086	6	1.944	25%
MD	4.810	8.5	1.767	20%
NC	6.252	11	1.760	18%
UT	1.592	2	1.256	13%
GA	5.971	7	1.172	35%
OR	2.737	3	1.096	14%
TN	4.734	5	1.056	19%
IN	5.518	5	0.906	5%
NY	17.774	15	0.844	10%
OH	10.822	9	0.832	14%
KS	2.421	2	0.826	6%
KY	3.673	3	0.817	9%
PA	11.875	9	0.758	10%
MI	9.255	7	0.756	14%
IL	11.681	8	0.685	7%
CT	3.197	2	0.626	14%
AZ	3.202	2	0.625	33%
MO	5.017	3	0.598	8%
MA	5.877	3	0.511	15%
TX	15.608	7	0.449	15%
AR	2.318	1	0.431	7%
CO	3.092	1	0.323	10%
SC	3.303	1	0.303	17%
CA	26.715	7	0.262	7%
AL	3.966	1	0.252	8%
FL	11.339	2	0.176	10%
NJ	7.547	1	0.133	2%
HI	1.047			
IA	2.846			
LA	4.212			
ME	1.177			
MN	4.226			
NE	1.574			
NH	1.015			
NM	1.407			
NV	1.001			
WA	4.499			
WI	4.799			
WV	1.872			
DC	0.623	5	8.032	28%
AK	0.475			
DE	0.631			
ID	0.976			
MT	0.793			
ND	0.647			
RI	0.976			
SD	0.693			
VT	0.538			
WY	0.463			
UN				
XX		1		6%
TOT	234.0	150	0.684	11%

Number of Players Selected

State	Pop (M)	#	Con	%
MS	2.547	4	1.571	57%
VA	6.078	8.5	1.399	32%
UT	1.592	2	1.256	20%
MD	4.810	5.5	1.144	15%
NC	6.252	7	1.120	18%
OR	2.737	3	1.096	14%
GA	5.971	6	1.005	33%
OK	3.086	3	0.972	16%
KS	2.421	2	0.826	8%
KY	3.673	3	0.817	13%
OH	10.822	8	0.739	17%
IN	5.518	4	0.725	6%
NY	17.774	11	0.675	11%
MI	9.255	6	0.648	15%
IL	11.681	7	0.599	8%
MO	5.017	3	0.598	12%
PA	11.875	7	0.589	11%
TX	15.608	7	0.449	14%
AR	2.318	1	0.431	8%
TN	4.734	2	0.422	10%
CT	3.197	1	0.313	10%
AZ	3.202	1	0.312	25%
SC	3.303	1	0.303	20%
CA	26.715	7	0.262	9%
FL	11.339	2	0.176	12%
MA	5.877	1	0.170	8%
NJ	7.547	1	0.133	3%
CO	3.092			
HI	1.047			
IA	2.846			
LA	4.212			
ME	1.177			
MN	4.226			
NE	1.574			
NH	1.015			
NM	1.407			
NV	1.001			
WA	4.499			
WI	4.799			
WV	1.872			
DC	0.623	3	4.819	23%
AK	0.475			
DE	0.631			
ID	0.976			
MT	0.793			
ND	0.647			
RI	0.976			
SD	0.693			
VT	0.538			
WY	0.463			
UN				
XX		1		7%
TOT	234.0	117	0.530	11%

SO-4: Concentration of NCAA All-Americans by Decade

1990-1999

Number of Selections

State	Pop (M)	#	Con	%
IN	5.984	11	1.838	10%
OK	3.417	5	1.463	21%
VA	7.337	10	1.363	26%
AR	2.620	3	1.145	20%
MI	9.610	11	1.145	22%
MD	5.542	5	0.902	12%
PA	12.244	11	0.898	12%
TN	5.587	5	0.895	19%
NJ	8.219	7	0.852	16%
MS	2.763	2	0.724	22%
NY	18.766	13	0.693	9%
IA	2.893	2	0.691	10%
NC	8.005	5	0.625	8%
NE	1.688	1	0.593	14%
CA	33.361	18	0.540	18%
SC	4.024	2	0.497	33%
CO	4.160	2	0.481	22%
LA	4.356	2	0.459	10%
TX	20.885	8	0.383	17%
MA	6.305	2	0.317	10%
OR	3.334	1	0.300	5%
CT	3.403	1	0.294	7%
OH	11.195	3	0.268	5%
KY	4.000	1	0.250	3%
GA	8.154	2	0.245	11%
AL	4.375	1	0.229	8%
AZ	5.141	1	0.195	17%
FL	15.738	3	0.191	15%
WI	5.274	1	0.190	4%
MO	5.553	1	0.180	4%
WA	5.766	1	0.173	6%
IL	12.427	2	0.161	2%
HI	1.202			
ID	1.277			
KS	2.649			
ME	1.273			
MN	4.821			
NH	1.217			
NM	1.763			
NV	1.923			
RI	1.028			
UT	2.254			
WV	1.807			
DC	0.604	2	3.314	11%
AK	0.624	2	3.205	67%
DE	0.776			
MT	0.887			
ND	0.643			
SD	0.754			
VT	0.593			
WY	0.499			
UN				
XX		5		31%
TOT	276.9	150	0.542	10%

Number of Players Selected

State	Pop (M)	#	Con	%
OK	3.417	4	1.171	21%
IN	5.984	7	1.170	10%
VA	7.337	7	0.954	26%
MD	5.542	5	0.902	14%
MI	9.610	8	0.832	21%
AR	2.620	2	0.763	15%
NJ	8.219	6	0.730	17%
TN	5.587	4	0.716	20%
NE	1.688	1	0.593	20%
NY	18.766	11	0.586	10%
PA	12.244	7	0.572	11%
NC	8.005	4	0.500	11%
CO	4.160	2	0.481	33%
CA	33.361	16	0.480	20%
MS	2.763	1	0.362	14%
IA	2.893	1	0.346	7%
MA	6.305	2	0.317	15%
OR	3.334	1	0.300	5%
CT	3.403	1	0.294	10%
TX	20.885	6	0.287	14%
KY	4.000	1	0.250	4%
SC	4.024	1	0.249	20%
GA	8.154	2	0.245	11%
LA	4.356	1	0.230	7%
AL	4.375	1	0.229	10%
AZ	5.141	1	0.195	25%
FL	15.738	3	0.191	18%
WI	5.274	1	0.190	5%
MO	5.553	1	0.180	4%
OH	11.195	2	0.179	4%
WA	5.766	1	0.173	6%
IL	12.427	2	0.161	2%
HI	1.202			
ID	1.277			
KS	2.649			
ME	1.273			
MN	4.821			
NH	1.217			
NM	1.763			
NV	1.923			
RI	1.028			
UT	2.254			
WV	1.807			
DC	0.604	2	3.314	15%
AK	0.624	1	1.603	50%
DE	0.776			
MT	0.887			
ND	0.643			
SD	0.754			
VT	0.593			
WY	0.499			
UN				
XX		3		21%
TOT	276.9	117	0.424	10%

2000-2009

Number of Selections

State	Pop (M)	#	Con	%
MD	6.037	11	1.822	26%
LA	4.513	7	1.551	33%
IN	6.453	9	1.395	8%
OR	3.829	5	1.306	24%
IA	3.027	3	0.991	15%
IL	12.870	12	0.932	11%
WA	6.694	6	0.896	35%
NC	9.458	8	0.846	13%
MO	5.988	5	0.835	13%
OK	3.719	3	0.807	13%
MI	9.927	8	0.806	16%
KS	2.836	2	0.705	6%
NJ	8.750	6	0.686	14%
CT	3.546	2	0.564	7%
PA	12.654	6	0.474	7%
KY	4.327	2	0.462	6%
TX	24.964	11	0.441	23%
AL	4.744	2	0.422	15%
CO	5.027	2	0.398	13%
MN	5.285	2	0.378	13%
CA	37.108	14	0.377	14%
WI	5.671	2	0.353	8%
TN	6.321	2	0.316	7%
GA	9.758	3	0.307	10%
MA	6.571	2	0.304	10%
VA	8.242	2	0.243	5%
SC	4.593	1	0.218	17%
NY	19.460	4	0.206	3%
OH	11.540	2	0.173	3%
FL	18.670	2	0.107	10%
AR	2.902			
AZ	6.494			
HI	1.328			
ID	1.557			
ME	1.323			
MS	2.960			
NE	1.812			
NH	1.321			
NM	2.035			
NV	2.672			
RI	1.053			
UT	2.774			
WV	1.836			
AK	0.704	1	1.420	33%
DC	0.601			
DE	0.891			
MT	0.982			
ND	0.660			
SD	0.813			
VT	0.624			
WY	0.554			
UN				
XX		3		19%
TOT	306.4	150	0.507	10%

Number of Players Selected

State	Pop (M)	#	Con	%
MD	6.037	11	1.822	30%
LA	4.513	7	1.551	47%
OR	3.829	5	1.306	24%
IN	6.453	7	1.085	10%
IA	3.027	3	0.991	15%
WA	6.694	6	0.896	38%
IL	12.870	11	0.855	13%
NC	9.458	6	0.634	16%
MI	9.927	6	0.604	15%
OK	3.719	2	0.538	11%
NJ	8.750	4	0.457	11%
TX	24.964	11	0.441	26%
AL	4.744	2	0.422	15%
PA	12.654	5	0.395	8%
WI	5.671	2	0.353	9%
KS	2.836	1	0.353	4%
MO	5.988	2	0.334	8%
CA	37.108	12	0.323	15%
TN	6.321	2	0.316	10%
GA	9.758	3	0.307	17%
KY	4.327	1	0.231	4%
SC	4.593	1	0.218	20%
NY	19.460	4	0.206	4%
CO	5.027	1	0.199	7%
MN	5.285	1	0.189	8%
OH	11.540	2	0.173	4%
MA	6.571	1	0.152	8%
VA	8.242	1	0.121	4%
FL	18.670	2	0.107	12%
AR	2.902			
AZ	6.494			
HI	1.328			
ID	1.557			
ME	1.323			
MS	2.960			
NE	1.812			
NH	1.321			
NM	2.035			
NV	2.672			
RI	1.053			
UT	2.774			
WV	1.836			
AK	0.704	1	1.420	50%
DC	0.601			
DE	0.891			
MT	0.982			
ND	0.660			
SD	0.813			
VT	0.624			
WY	0.554			
UN				
XX		3		21%
TOT	306.4	128	0.433	12%

2010-2016

Number of Selections

State	Pop (M)	#	Con	%
CA	37.254	8	0.215	8%
NH	1.316	4	3.038	100%
IA	3.046	5	1.641	25%
KS	2.853	4	1.402	11%
NV	2.701	3	1.111	75%
IN	6.484	7	1.080	6%
MD	6.074	6.5	1.070	15%
AR	2.916	3	1.029	20%
RI	1.053	1	0.950	33%
IL	12.831	10	0.779	9%
NJ	8.792	6	0.682	14%
MO	5.989	4	0.668	11%
MN	5.304	3	0.566	19%
VA	8.302	4.5	0.542	12%
GA	9.688	4	0.413	20%
NY	19.378	8	0.413	6%
OH	11.537	4	0.347	6%
MS	2.967	1	0.337	11%
NC	9.535	3	0.315	5%
MI	9.884	3	0.304	6%
CT	3.574	1	0.280	7%
FL	18.801	5	0.266	25%
OR	3.831	1	0.261	5%
TX	25.146	6	0.239	13%
LA	4.533	1	0.221	5%
SC	4.625	1	0.216	17%
AL	4.780	1	0.209	8%
TN	6.346	1	0.158	4%
PA	12.702	2	0.157	2%
AZ	6.392	1	0.156	17%
MA	6.548	1	0.153	5%
CO	5.029			
HI	1.360			
ID	1.568			
KY	4.339			
ME	1.328			
NE	1.826			
NM	2.059			
OK	3.751			
UT	2.764			
WA	6.725			
WI	5.687			
WV	1.853			
DC	0.602	1	1.662	6%
AK	0.704			
DE	0.891			
MT	0.982			
ND	0.660			
SD	0.813			
VT	0.624			
WY	0.554			
UN				
XX		7		44%
TOT	305.6	120	0.395	8%

Number of Players Selected

State	Pop (M)	#	Con	%
NH	1.316	4	3.038	100%
NV	2.701	3	1.111	75%
MD	6.074	6.5	1.070	18%
KS	2.853	3	1.051	13%
AR	2.916	3	1.029	23%
IA	3.046	3	0.985	20%
RI	1.053	1	0.950	33%
IN	6.484	6	0.925	8%
IL	12.831	9	0.701	11%
NJ	8.792	6	0.682	17%
MO	5.989	4	0.668	16%
MN	5.304	3	0.566	25%
VA	8.302	4.5	0.542	17%
GA	9.688	4	0.413	22%
NY	19.378	7	0.361	7%
MS	2.967	1	0.337	14%
NC	9.535	3	0.315	8%
MI	9.884	3	0.304	8%
CT	3.574	1	0.280	10%
FL	18.801	5	0.266	29%
OR	3.831	1	0.261	5%
OH	11.537	3	0.260	7%
TX	25.146	6	0.239	14%
LA	4.533	1	0.221	7%
SC	4.625	1	0.216	20%
CA	37.254	8	0.215	10%
AL	4.780	1	0.209	10%
TN	6.346	1	0.158	5%
PA	12.702	2	0.157	3%
AZ	6.392	1	0.156	25%
MA	6.548	1	0.153	8%
CO	5.029			
HI	1.360			
ID	1.568			
KY	4.339			
ME	1.328			
NE	1.826			
NM	2.059			
OK	3.751			
UT	2.764			
WA	6.725			
WI	5.687			
WV	1.853			
DC	0.602	1	1.662	8%
AK	0.710			
DE	0.898			
MT	0.989			
ND	0.673			
SD	0.814			
VT	0.626			
WY	0.564			
UN				
XX		7		50%
TOT	305.6	113	0.364	10%

SO-5: Concentration of NBA Coaches by Games Coached

1+ GC

State	Pop (M)	#	Con
IN	5.149	29	5.632
NY	17.230	53	3.076
NJ	6.860	19	2.769
WV	1.873	5	2.669
LA	3.679	9	2.447
IL	10.867	24	2.209
PA	11.575	24	2.073
OH	9.997	20	2.001
KY	3.509	7	1.995
ME	1.091	2	1.834
CT	2.848	5	1.756
MD	4.303	7	1.627
CA	22.620	35	1.547
KS	2.332	3	1.286
OR	2.452	3	1.223
NC	6.087	7	1.150
WI	4.489	5	1.114
VA	5.588	6	1.074
MN	4.005	4	0.999
MI	8.346	8	0.959
NV	1.049	1	0.953
MO	4.844	4	0.826
MS	2.470	2	0.810
NM	1.260	1	0.794
MA	5.595	4	0.715
IA	2.811	2	0.711
OK	2.879	2	0.695
UT	1.492	1	0.670
GA	5.821	3	0.515
WA	4.098	2	0.488
AR	2.251	1	0.444
CO	2.833	1	0.353
AZ	2.967	1	0.337
SC	3.099	1	0.323
TX	14.515	4	0.276
AL	3.754	1	0.266
TN	4.479	1	0.223
FL	9.560	2	0.209
NE	1.539		
DC	0.680	4	5.879
AK	0.396	1	2.527
WY	0.405	1	2.469
RI	0.919	2	2.175
VT	0.487	1	2.054
ND	0.640	1	1.562
MT	0.760	1	1.316
NH	0.880	1	1.136
HI	0.893	1	1.120
ID	0.946	1	1.057
DE	0.579		
SD	0.707		
UN		3	
XX		1	
TOT		323	

100+ GC

State	Pop (M)	#	Con	%
IN	5.149	16	3.107	55%
NY	17.230	38	2.205	72%
WV	1.873	4	2.135	80%
PA	11.575	22	1.901	92%
NJ	6.860	13	1.895	68%
ME	1.091	2	1.834	100%
KY	3.509	6	1.710	86%
MD	4.303	6.5	1.510	93%
IL	10.867	16	1.472	67%
LA	3.679	5	1.359	56%
OH	9.997	11	1.100	55%
CT	2.848	3	1.053	60%
CA	22.620	22	0.973	63%
NV	1.049	1	0.953	100%
KS	2.332	2	0.858	67%
OR	2.452	2	0.816	67%
MN	4.005	3	0.749	75%
UT	1.492	1	0.670	100%
WI	4.489	3	0.668	60%
NC	6.087	4	0.657	57%
VA	5.588	3.5	0.626	58%
MO	4.844	3	0.619	75%
MA	5.595	3	0.536	75%
WA	4.098	2	0.488	100%
MI	8.346	4	0.479	50%
MS	2.470	1	0.405	50%
IA	2.811	1	0.356	50%
OK	2.879	1	0.347	50%
AZ	2.967	1	0.337	100%
SC	3.099	1	0.323	100%
TN	4.479	1	0.223	100%
GA	5.821	1	0.172	33%
FL	9.560	1	0.105	50%
TX	14.515	1	0.069	25%
AL	3.754			
AR	2.251			
CO	2.833			
NE	1.539			
NM	1.260			
DC	0.680	3	4.410	75%
VT	0.487	1	2.054	100%
ND	0.640	1	1.562	100%
MT	0.760	1	1.316	100%
HI	0.893	1	1.120	100%
RI	0.919	1	1.088	50%
ID	0.946	1	1.057	100%
AK	0.396			
DE	0.579			
NH	0.880			
SD	0.707			
WY	0.405			
UN				
XX		1		100%
TOT		212		66%

200+ GC

State	Pop (M)	#	Con	%
IN	5.149	10	1.942	34%
ME	1.091	2	1.834	100%
NY	17.230	28	1.625	53%
WV	1.873	3	1.602	60%
NJ	6.860	10	1.458	53%
MD	4.303	6	1.394	86%
LA	3.679	5	1.359	56%
PA	11.575	15	1.296	63%
KY	3.509	4	1.140	57%
CT	2.848	3	1.053	60%
IL	10.867	11	1.012	46%
NV	1.049	1	0.953	100%
OR	2.452	2	0.816	67%
OH	9.997	8	0.800	40%
MN	4.005	3	0.749	75%
UT	1.492	1	0.670	100%
CA	22.620	14	0.619	40%
NC	6.087	3	0.493	43%
WA	4.098	2	0.488	100%
WI	4.489	2	0.446	40%
KS	2.332	1	0.429	33%
MS	2.470	1	0.405	50%
MI	8.346	3	0.359	38%
VA	5.588	2	0.358	33%
IA	2.811	1	0.356	50%
AZ	2.967	1	0.337	100%
SC	3.099	1	0.323	100%
MO	4.844	1	0.206	25%
MA	5.595	1	0.179	25%
GA	5.821	1	0.172	33%
AL	3.754			
AR	2.251			
CO	2.833			
FL	9.560			
NE	1.539			
NM	1.260			
OK	2.879			
TN	4.479			
TX	14.515			
DC	0.680	2	2.940	50%
VT	0.487	1	2.054	100%
ND	0.640	1	1.562	100%
ID	0.946	1	1.057	100%
AK	0.396			
DE	0.579			
HI	0.893			
MT	0.760			
NH	0.880			
RI	0.919			
SD	0.707			
WY	0.405			
UN				
XX		1		100%
TOT		150		47%

300+ GC

State	Pop (M)	#	Con	%
IN	5.149	8	1.554	28%
NY	17.230	23	1.335	43%
NJ	6.860	9	1.312	47%
KY	3.509	4	1.140	57%
WV	1.873	2	1.068	40%
MD	4.303	4.5	1.046	64%
PA	11.575	12	1.037	50%
NV	1.049	1	0.953	100%
MN	4.005	3	0.749	75%
IL	10.867	8	0.736	33%
CT	2.848	2	0.702	40%
UT	1.492	1	0.670	100%
OH	9.997	6	0.600	30%
LA	3.679	2	0.544	22%
NC	6.087	3	0.493	43%
CA	22.620	10	0.442	29%
KS	2.332	1	0.429	33%
OR	2.452	1	0.408	33%
MS	2.470	1	0.405	50%
IA	2.811	1	0.356	50%
AZ	2.967	1	0.337	100%
VA	5.588	1.5	0.268	25%
WI	4.489	1	0.223	20%
MO	4.844	1	0.206	25%
MA	5.595	1	0.179	25%
GA	5.821	1	0.172	33%
MI	8.346	1	0.120	13%
AL	3.754			
AR	2.251			
CO	2.833			
FL	9.560			
ME	1.091			
NE	1.539			
NM	1.260			
OK	2.879			
SC	3.099			
TN	4.479			
TX	14.515			
WA	4.098			
VT	0.487	1	2.054	100%
ND	0.640	1	1.562	100%
DC	0.680	1	1.470	25%
ID	0.946	1	1.057	100%
AK	0.396			
DE	0.579			
HI	0.893			
MT	0.760			
NH	0.880			
RI	0.919			
SD	0.707			
WY	0.405			
UN				
XX				
TOT		113		35%

SO-5: Concentration of NBA Coaches by Games Coached

400+ GC

State	Pop (M)	#	Con	%
IN	5.149	8	1.554	28%
NJ	6.860	9	1.312	47%
NY	17.230	19	1.103	36%
WV	1.873	2	1.068	40%
NV	1.049	1	0.953	100%
PA	11.575	10	0.864	42%
KY	3.509	3	0.855	43%
UT	1.492	1	0.670	100%
IL	10.867	7	0.644	29%
MD	4.303	3	0.581	36%
LA	3.679	2	0.544	22%
MN	4.005	2	0.499	50%
NC	6.087	3	0.493	43%
CA	22.620	10	0.442	29%
OR	2.452	1	0.408	33%
OH	9.997	4	0.400	20%
IA	2.811	1	0.356	50%
CT	2.848	1	0.351	20%
VA	5.588	2	0.268	25%
WI	4.489	1	0.223	20%
MO	4.844	1	0.206	25%
MA	5.595	1	0.179	25%
MI	8.346	1	0.120	13%
AL	3.754			
AR	2.251			
AZ	2.967			
CO	2.833			
FL	9.560			
GA	5.821			
KS	2.332			
ME	1.091			
MS	2.470			
NE	1.539			
NM	1.260			
OK	2.879			
SC	3.099			
TN	4.479			
TX	14.515			
WA	4.098			
ND	0.640	1	1.562	100%
DC	0.680	1	1.470	25%
ID	0.946	1	1.057	100%
AK	0.396			
DE	0.579			
HI	0.893			
MT	0.760			
NH	0.880			
RI	0.919			
SD	0.707			
VT	0.487			
WY	0.405			
UN				
XX				
TOT		94		29%

500+ GC

State	Pop (M)	#	Con	%
IN	5.149	7	1.359	24%
NJ	6.860	9	1.312	47%
WV	1.873	2	1.068	40%
NY	17.230	16	0.929	30%
KY	3.509	3	0.855	43%
PA	11.575	9	0.778	38%
UT	1.492	1	0.670	100%
MD	4.303	2.5	0.581	36%
IL	10.867	6	0.552	25%
CA	22.620	10	0.442	29%
OR	2.452	1	0.408	33%
OH	9.997	4	0.400	20%
IA	2.811	1	0.356	50%
NC	6.087	2	0.329	29%
LA	3.679	1	0.272	11%
MN	4.005	1	0.250	25%
WI	4.489	1	0.223	20%
MO	4.844	1	0.206	25%
MI	8.346	1	0.120	13%
VA	5.588	0.5	0.089	8%
AL	3.754			
AR	2.251			
AZ	2.967			
CO	2.833			
CT	2.848			
FL	9.560			
GA	5.821			
KS	2.332			
MA	5.595			
ME	1.091			
MS	2.470			
NE	1.539			
NM	1.260			
NV	1.049			
OK	2.879			
SC	3.099			
TN	4.479			
TX	14.515			
WA	4.098			
ND	0.640	1	1.562	100%
DC	0.680	1	1.470	25%
ID	0.946	1	1.057	100%
AK	0.396			
DE	0.579			
HI	0.893			
MT	0.760			
NH	0.880			
RI	0.919			
SD	0.707			
VT	0.487			
WY	0.405			
UN				
XX				
TOT		81		25%

600+ GC

State	Pop (M)	#	Con	%
IN	5.149	7	1.359	24%
NJ	6.860	7	1.020	37%
NY	17.230	12	0.696	23%
UT	1.492	1	0.670	100%
MD	4.303	2.5	0.581	36%
WV	1.873	1	0.534	20%
IL	10.867	5	0.460	21%
PA	11.575	5	0.432	21%
OR	2.452	1	0.408	33%
IA	2.811	1	0.356	50%
CA	22.620	8	0.354	23%
NC	6.087	2	0.329	29%
KY	3.509	1	0.285	14%
LA	3.679	1	0.272	11%
MN	4.005	1	0.250	25%
WI	4.489	1	0.223	20%
MO	4.844	1	0.206	25%
OH	9.997	2	0.200	10%
MI	8.346	1	0.120	13%
VA	5.588	0.5	0.089	8%
AL	3.754			
AR	2.251			
AZ	2.967			
CO	2.833			
CT	2.848			
FL	9.560			
GA	5.821			
KS	2.332			
MA	5.595			
ME	1.091			
MS	2.470			
NE	1.539			
NM	1.260			
NV	1.049			
OK	2.879			
SC	3.099			
TN	4.479			
TX	14.515			
WA	4.098			
ND	0.640	1	1.562	100%
DC	0.680	1	1.470	25%
AK	0.396			
DE	0.579			
HI	0.893			
ID	0.946			
MT	0.760			
NH	0.880			
RI	0.919			
SD	0.707			
VT	0.487			
WY	0.405			
UN				
XX				
TOT		62		19%

700+ GC

State	Pop (M)	#	Con	%
IN	5.149	4	0.777	14%
UT	1.492	1	0.670	100%
NY	17.230	10	0.580	19%
WV	1.873	1	0.534	20%
MD	4.303	2	0.465	29%
NJ	6.860	3	0.437	16%
OR	2.452	1	0.408	33%
IL	10.867	4	0.368	17%
IA	2.811	1	0.356	50%
PA	11.575	4	0.346	17%
NC	6.087	2	0.329	29%
KY	3.509	1	0.285	14%
LA	3.679	1	0.272	11%
CA	22.620	6	0.265	17%
MN	4.005	1	0.250	25%
MO	4.844	1	0.206	25%
MI	8.346	1	0.120	13%
OH	9.997	1	0.100	5%
AL	3.754			
AR	2.251			
AZ	2.967			
CO	2.833			
CT	2.848			
FL	9.560			
GA	5.821			
KS	2.332			
MA	5.595			
ME	1.091			
MS	2.470			
NE	1.539			
NM	1.260			
NV	1.049			
OK	2.879			
SC	3.099			
TN	4.479			
TX	14.515			
VA	5.588			
WA	4.098			
WI	4.489			
ND	0.640	1	1.562	100%
AK	0.396			
DC	0.680			
DE	0.579			
HI	0.893			
ID	0.946			
MT	0.760			
NH	0.880			
RI	0.919			
SD	0.707			
VT	0.487			
WY	0.405			
UN				
XX				
TOT		46		14%

SO-5: Concentration of NBA Coaches by Games Coached

800+ GC					900+ GC					1000+ GC				
State	Pop (M)	#	Con	%	State	Pop (M)	#	Con	%	State	Pop (M)	#	Con	%
IN	5.149	4	0.777	14%	UT	1.492	1	0.670	100%	UT	1.492	1	0.670	100%
UT	1.492	1	0.670	100%	IN	5.149	3	0.583	10%	IN	5.149	3	0.583	10%
WV	1.873	1	0.534	20%	WV	1.873	1	0.534	20%	MD	4.303	2	0.465	29%
MD	4.303	2	0.465	29%	MD	3.963	2	0.505	29%	NY	17.230	8	0.464	15%
NY	17.230	8	0.464	15%	NY	17.230	8	0.464	15%	IA	2.811	1	0.356	50%
NJ	6.860	3	0.437	16%	NJ	6.860	3	0.437	16%	NJ	6.860	2	0.292	11%
IL	10.867	4	0.368	17%	IA	2.811	1	0.356	50%	IL	10.867	3	0.276	13%
IA	2.811	1	0.356	50%	KY	3.509	1	0.285	14%	PA	11.575	3	0.259	13%
KY	3.509	1	0.285	14%	IL	10.867	3	0.276	13%	MO	4.844	1	0.206	25%
LA	3.679	1	0.272	11%	PA	11.575	3	0.259	13%	NC	6.087	1	0.164	14%
PA	11.575	3	0.259	13%	MO	4.844	1	0.206	25%	OH	9.997	1	0.100	5%
CA	22.620	5	0.221	14%	NC	6.087	1	0.164	14%	CA	22.620	2	0.088	6%
MO	4.844	1	0.206	25%	MI	8.346	1	0.120	13%	AL	3.754			
NC	6.087	1	0.164	14%	OH	9.997	1	0.100	5%	AR	2.251			
MI	8.346	1	0.120	13%	CA	22.620	2	0.088	6%	AZ	2.967			
OH	9.997	1	0.100	5%	AL	3.754				CO	2.833			
AL	3.754				AR	2.251				CT	2.848			
AR	2.251				AZ	2.967				FL	9.560			
AZ	2.967				CO	2.833				GA	5.821			
CO	2.833				CT	2.848				KS	2.332			
CT	2.848				FL	9.560				KY	3.509			
FL	9.560				GA	5.821				LA	3.679			
GA	5.821				KS	2.332				MA	5.595			
KS	2.332				LA	3.679				ME	1.091			
MA	5.595				MA	5.595				MI	8.346			
ME	1.091				ME	1.091				MN	4.005			
MN	4.005				MN	4.005				MS	2.470			
MS	2.470				MS	2.470				NE	1.539			
NE	1.539				NE	1.539				NM	1.260			
NM	1.260				NM	1.260				NV	1.049			
NV	1.049				NV	1.049				OK	2.879			
OK	2.879				OK	2.879				OR	2.452			
OR	2.452				OR	2.452				SC	3.099			
SC	3.099				SC	3.099				TN	4.479			
TN	4.479				TN	4.479				TX	14.515			
TX	14.515				TX	14.515				VA	5.588			
VA	5.588				VA	5.248				WA	4.098			
WA	4.098				WA	4.098				WI	4.489			
WI	4.489				WI	4.489				WV	1.873			
ND	0.640	1	1.562	100%	ND	0.640	1	1.562	100%	ND	0.640	1	1.562	100%
AK	0.396				AK	0.396				AK	0.396			
DC	0.680				DC	0.680				DC	0.680			
DE	0.579				DE	0.579				DE	0.579			
HI	0.893				HI	0.893				HI	0.893			
ID	0.946				ID	0.946				ID	0.946			
MT	0.760				MT	0.760				MT	0.760			
NH	0.880				NH	0.880				NH	0.880			
RI	0.919				RI	0.919				RI	0.919			
SD	0.707				SD	0.707				SD	0.707			
VT	0.487				VT	0.487				VT	0.487			
WY	0.405				WY	0.405				WY	0.405			
UN					UN					UN				
XX					XX					XX				
TOT		39		12%	TOT		33		10%	TOT		29		9%

SO-6: Concentration of NCAA Division I Coaches by Decade

All Years				1895-1929					1930-1949					1950-1959					1960-1969				
State	Pop (M)	#	Con	State	Pop (M)	#	Con	%	State	Pop (M)	#	Con	%	State	Pop (M)	#	Con	%	State	Pop (M)	#	Con	%
IN	4.045	107	26.455	IN	2.847	16	5.621	15%	IN	3.540	18	5.085	17%	OK	2.263	6	2.651	21%	OK	2.446	7	2.862	25%
UT	1.042	22	21.121	KS	1.703	7	4.111	19%	KS	1.866	8	4.288	22%	OR	1.653	3	1.815	23%	IN	4.936	11	2.229	10%
KS	1.959	36	18.376	IA	2.333	8	3.430	23%	NE	1.339	3	2.240	50%	WV	1.932	3	1.553	13%	KY	3.134	5	1.595	10%
KY	2.888	51	17.662	PA	8.080	26	3.218	19%	TX	6.663	14	2.101	19%	IA	2.691	4	1.486	11%	KS	2.214	3	1.355	8%
WV	1.566	24	15.326	MN	2.195	6	2.734	38%	IA	2.543	5	1.966	14%	KS	2.047	3	1.466	8%	TN	3.750	5	1.334	22%
IA	2.448	35	14.299	MD	1.583	4	2.527	11%	OH	7.167	13	1.814	14%	OH	8.843	12	1.357	13%	SC	2.492	3	1.204	17%
PA	9.609	135	14.049	MA	3.568	8	2.242	18%	CO	1.165	2	1.716	22%	CT	2.278	3	1.317	13%	OH	10.198	12	1.177	13%
MS	2.070	28	13.526	NY	9.839	21	2.134	12%	OR	1.192	2	1.678	15%	VA	4.014	5	1.246	10%	WV	1.801	2	1.111	8%
VA	4.163	56	13.451	VA	2.353	5	2.125	9%	AR	1.903	3	1.576	21%	PA	10.921	13	1.190	10%	IA	2.793	3	1.074	9%
NY	13.631	179	13.132	OH	5.333	11	2.063	11%	SC	1.919	3	1.563	17%	IN	4.315	5	1.159	5%	PA	11.572	11	0.951	8%
NC	4.502	59	13.105	MI	3.435	7	2.038	14%	KY	2.806	4	1.426	8%	WI	3.707	4	1.079	15%	NY	17.534	16	0.913	9%
IL	8.578	108	12.591	IL	6.144	12	1.953	11%	GA	3.161	4	1.265	17%	KY	3.002	3	0.999	6%	NJ	6.635	6	0.904	10%
LA	2.797	35	12.512	WA	1.145	2	1.747	12%	NY	13.632	16	1.174	9%	MO	4.139	4	0.967	15%	TX	10.408	9	0.865	13%
OH	7.793	97	12.448	MO	3.358	5	1.489	19%	IL	8.080	9	1.114	8%	AZ	1.037	1	0.964	13%	CA	17.911	15	0.837	14%
OK	2.300	28	12.173	SC	1.570	2	1.274	11%	MI	5.506	6	1.090	12%	IL	9.413	9	0.956	8%	MN	3.616	3	0.830	19%
MD	3.135	36	11.482	KY	2.367	3	1.267	6%	WA	1.895	2	1.055	12%	TX	8.683	7	0.806	10%	VA	4.694	3.5	0.746	6%
NJ	5.116	58	11.338	WI	2.493	3	1.203	12%	AL	2.846	3	1.054	12%	NJ	5.480	4	0.730	7%	MO	4.505	3	0.666	11%
CT	2.138	23	10.758	OK	1.718	2	1.164	7%	WV	1.899	2	1.053	8%	NY	15.829	10	0.632	6%	IL	10.612	7	0.660	6%
MA	4.541	44	9.690	LA	1.735	2	1.153	6%	FL	2.062	2	0.970	9%	GA	3.700	2	0.541	9%	AZ	1.547	1	0.647	13%
AL	2.999	26	8.668	CA	3.242	3	0.925	3%	MS	2.121	2	0.943	7%	CA	13.218	7	0.530	6%	WA	3.137	2	0.638	12%
MI	6.193	51	8.235	TX	4.358	4	0.918	6%	CA	7.724	7	0.906	6%	NC	4.312	2	0.464	3%	AL	3.359	2	0.596	8%
SC	2.390	18	7.531	TN	2.290	2	0.873	9%	MN	2.784	2	0.718	13%	MI	7.135	1	0.140	2%	AR	1.856	1	0.539	7%
AR	1.885	14	7.429	NC	2.457	2	0.814	3%	PA	10.010	7	0.699	5%	AL	3.167				MS	2.199	1	0.455	4%
WI	3.529	26	7.367	CT	1.253	1	0.798	4%	TN	2.946	2	0.679	9%	AR	1.847				NC	4.824	2	0.415	3%
CA	14.917	109	7.307	WV	1.343	1	0.744	4%	VA	3.115	2	0.642	4%	CO	1.548				MD	3.900	1.5	0.385	4%
TX	10.273	72	7.008	NJ	2.905	2	0.689	3%	WI	3.175	2	0.630	8%	FL	3.886				MA	5.428	2	0.368	5%
MO	4.014	27	6.726	MS	1.787	1	0.560	4%	CT	1.774	1	0.564	4%	LA	2.986				WI	4.191	1	0.239	4%
TN	3.461	23	6.646	AL	2.240				NC	3.601	2	0.555	3%	MA	4.929				GA	4.269	1	0.234	4%
WA	2.874	17	5.915	AR	1.623				MO	3.787	2	0.528	7%	MD	3.140				FL	5.871	1	0.170	4%
OR	2.300	13	5.652	GA	2.657				OK	2.308	1	0.433	4%	MN	3.211				MI	8.365	1	0.120	2%
GA	4.400	23	5.227	NE	3.916				NJ	4.354	1	0.230	2%	NE	1.369				CO	1.984			
MN	3.140	16	5.096						MA	4.419	1	0.226	2%	SC	2.256				CT	2.790			
CO	1.998	9	4.503						LA	2.389				TN	3.439				LA	3.458			
AZ	1.910	8	4.187						MD	2.270				WA	2.623				NE	1.450			
FL	6.169	23	3.728																OR	1.933			
NE	2.152	6	2.788																				
DC	0.537	12	22.359	UT	0.402	6	14.931	27%	WY	0.256	1	3.903	25%	WY	0.312	1	3.205	25%	UT	0.978	3	3.069	14%
ID	0.687	11	16.012	ID	0.341	2	5.864	18%	NM	0.547	2	3.653	33%	ID	0.632	2	3.167	18%	ID	0.692	2	2.890	18%
WY	0.300	4	13.340	DC	0.384	2	5.214	17%	MT	0.565	2	3.541	29%	UT	0.796	2	2.513	9%	NH	0.674	1	1.485	20%
MT	0.599	7	11.689	NH	0.438	2	4.570	40%	ID	0.521	1	1.921	9%	RI	0.818	2	2.445	29%	DC	0.760	1	1.317	8%
ND	0.565	6	10.617	OR	0.706	3	4.250	23%	AZ	0.564	1	1.775	13%	SD	0.667	1	1.499	25%	RI	0.904	1	1.107	14%
RI	0.740	7	9.461	AZ	0.274	1	3.646	13%	ND	0.646	1	1.547	17%	NM	0.823	1	1.216	17%	NM	0.988	1	1.013	17%
ME	0.902	7	7.759	ND	0.556	1	1.799	17%	AK	0.112				AK	0.183				AK	0.266			
NH	0.676	5	7.393	ME	0.751	1	1.332	14%	DC	0.655				DC	0.788				DE	0.499			
NM	0.876	6	6.852	CO	0.829	1	1.207	11%	DE	0.275				DE	0.385				HI	0.706			
SD	0.613	4	6.524	AK	0.061				HI	0.450				HI	0.567				ME	0.984			
NV	0.668	2	2.993	DE	0.212				ME	0.852				ME	0.943				MT	0.686			
HI	0.624	1	1.602	FL	0.929				NH	0.496				MT	0.638				ND	0.626			
AK	0.262				HI	0.243				NV	0.121				ND	0.625				NV	0.389			
DE	0.421				MT	0.426				RI	0.726				NH	0.570				SD	0.674			
VT	0.408				NM	0.327				SD	0.663				NV	0.225				VT	0.418			
				NV	0.073				UT	0.585				VT	0.384				WY	0.332			
				RI	0.566				VT	0.365													
				SD	0.579																		
				VT	0.353																		
				WY	0.165																		
UN		21		UN		7		33%	UN		7		33%	UN		3		14%	UN		2		
XX		2		XX		2		100%	XX					XX					XX				
TOT	167	1725	10.321	TOT	102	192	2.967	11%	TOT	136	166	1.678	9%	TOT	166	125	1.600	7%	TOT	192	151	1.600	8%

SO-6: Concentration of NCAA Division I Coaches by Decade

1970-1979

State	Pop (M)	#	Con	%
KY	3.441	14	4.069	27%
ME	1.060	4	3.775	57%
WV	1.847	5	2.707	21%
CT	3.070	7	2.281	30%
OK	2.793	6	2.149	21%
LA	3.924	7	1.784	20%
MS	2.369	4	1.689	14%
IN	5.343	9	1.684	8%
NJ	7.268	12	1.651	21%
OH	10.727	16	1.492	16%
PA	11.834	17	1.437	13%
TN	4.259	6	1.409	26%
KS	2.306	3	1.301	8%
NC	5.479	7	1.278	12%
MD	4.419	5	1.132	14%
IL	11.265	12	1.065	11%
NY	17.899	19	1.062	11%
MO	4.798	5	1.042	19%
MI	9.071	9	0.992	18%
AR	2.104	2	0.951	14%
VA	5.347	5	0.935	9%
CA	21.820	19	0.871	17%
UT	1.260	1	0.794	5%
IA	2.870	2	0.697	6%
WI	4.562	3	0.658	12%
NE	1.528	1	0.655	17%
GA	5.026	3	0.597	13%
TX	12.714	7	0.551	10%
AL	3.668	2	0.545	14%
WA	3.772	2	0.530	12%
MA	5.713	3	0.525	7%
MN	3.942	2	0.507	13%
OR	2.362	1	0.423	8%
SC	2.855	1	0.350	6%
FL	8.265	2	0.242	9%
NM	1.158			
AZ	2.247			
CO	2.550			
ND	0.636	3	4.717	50%
ID	0.829	3	3.619	27%
DC	0.698	2	2.867	17%
WY	0.402	1	2.491	25%
SD	0.678	1	1.475	25%
RI	0.949	1	1.054	14%
AK	0.352			
DE	0.572			
HI	0.878			
MT	0.741			
NH	0.830			
NV	0.644			
VT	0.479			
UN		1		5%
XX				
TOT	216	233	1.600	13%

1980-1989

State	Pop (M)	#	Con	%
MS	2.547	8	3.378	29%
UT	1.592	4	3.175	18%
IN	5.518	14	2.620	13%
NC	6.252	13	2.373	22%
NJ	7.547	13	1.789	22%
LA	4.212	7	1.784	20%
AL	3.966	6	1.636	23%
NY	17.774	29	1.620	16%
PA	11.875	19	1.606	14%
IL	11.681	17	1.509	16%
AR	2.318	3	1.426	21%
MA	5.877	7	1.225	16%
NH	1.015	1	1.206	20%
GA	5.971	6	1.194	26%
KY	3.673	4	1.162	8%
MD	4.810	5.5	1.144	15%
WV	1.872	2	1.083	8%
VA	6.078	6.5	1.069	12%
SC	3.303	3	1.051	17%
KS	2.421	2	0.867	6%
FL	11.339	7	0.847	30%
OH	10.822	9	0.839	9%
MO	5.017	4	0.834	15%
CO	3.092	2	0.784	22%
TX	15.608	9	0.708	13%
IA	2.846	2	0.697	6%
WI	4.799	3	0.658	12%
CT	3.197	2	0.652	9%
MI	9.255	5	0.551	10%
CA	26.715	12	0.550	11%
TN	4.734	2	0.470	9%
AZ	3.202	1	0.445	13%
OR	2.737	1	0.423	8%
MN	4.226	1	0.254	6%
HI	1.047			
ME	1.177			
NE	1.574			
NM	1.407			
NV	1.001			
OK	3.086			
WA	4.499			
DC	0.623	1	1.434	8%
RI	0.976	1	1.054	14%
AK	0.475			
DE	0.631			
ID	0.976			
MT	0.793			
ND	0.647			
SD	0.693			
VT	0.538			
WY	0.463			
UN		1		5%
XX		0		
TOT	238	232	1.600	13%

1990-1999

State	Pop (M)	#	Con	%
LA	4.356	10	2.296	29%
UT	2.254	5	2.218	23%
MD	5.542	11.5	2.075	33%
IN	5.984	12	2.006	11%
VA	7.065	13.5	1.911	24%
MS	2.763	5	1.810	18%
WV	1.807	3	1.661	13%
NY	18.766	31	1.652	18%
ME	1.273	2	1.571	29%
PA	12.244	19	1.552	14%
KS	2.649	4	1.510	11%
KY	4.000	6	1.500	12%
NC	8.005	12	1.499	20%
NE	1.688	2	1.185	33%
IL	12.427	18	1.449	17%
OK	3.417	4	1.171	14%
NJ	8.219	9	1.095	16%
IA	2.893	3	1.037	9%
SC	4.024	4	0.994	22%
OH	11.195	11	0.983	11%
MA	6.305	6	0.952	14%
NH	1.217	1	0.822	20%
ID	1.277	1	0.783	9%
AR	2.620	2	0.763	14%
WI	5.274	4	0.759	15%
MI	9.610	7	0.728	14%
AL	4.375	3	0.686	12%
CA	33.361	22	0.659	20%
CT	3.403	2	0.588	9%
NM	1.763	1	0.567	17%
TX	20.885	8	0.383	11%
MO	5.553	2	0.360	7%
TN	5.587	2	0.358	9%
WA	5.766	2	0.347	12%
OR	3.334	1	0.300	8%
FL	15.738	4	0.254	17%
CO	4.160	1	0.240	11%
AZ	5.141	1	0.195	13%
GA	8.154	1	0.123	4%
HI	1.202			
MN	4.821			
NV	1.923			
RI	1.028			
DC	0.604	3	4.971	25%
MT	0.887	3	3.382	43%
WY	0.499	1	2.004	25%
SD	0.754	1	1.326	25%
AK	0.624			
DE	0.776			
ND	0.643			
VT	0.593			
UN				
XX				
TOT	278	261	1.600	15%

2000-2017

State	Pop (M)	#	Con	%
IN	6.453	22	3.409	21%
WV	1.836	6	3.267	25%
KY	4.327	12	2.773	24%
IA	3.027	8	2.643	23%
MA	6.571	17	2.587	39%
KS	2.836	6	2.116	17%
AL	4.744	10	2.108	38%
NC	9.458	19	2.009	32%
LA	4.513	9	1.994	26%
CT	3.546	7	1.974	30%
NY	19.460	37	1.901	21%
RI	1.053	2	1.900	29%
VA	8.242	15.5	1.881	28%
IL	12.870	24	1.865	22%
PA	12.654	23	1.818	17%
MS	2.960	5	1.689	18%
MI	9.927	15	1.511	29%
MD	6.037	8.5	1.408	24%
NJ	8.750	11	1.257	19%
OH	11.540	13	1.127	13%
WI	5.671	6	1.058	23%
WA	6.694	7	1.046	41%
AR	2.902	3	1.034	21%
HI	1.328	1	0.753	100%
NV	2.672	2	0.749	100%
CA	37.108	24	0.647	22%
TN	6.321	4	0.633	17%
GA	9.758	6	0.615	26%
CO	5.027	3	0.597	33%
TX	24.964	14	0.561	19%
OK	3.719	2	0.538	7%
OR	3.829	2	0.522	15%
NM	2.035	1	0.491	17%
SC	4.593	2	0.435	11%
MN	5.285	2	0.378	13%
FL	18.670	7	0.375	30%
UT	2.774	1	0.360	5%
MO	5.988	2	0.334	7%
AZ	6.494	2	0.308	25%
ID	1.557			
ME	1.323			
NE	1.812			
NH	1.321			
DC	0.601	3	4.993	25%
MT	0.982	2	2.036	29%
ND	0.660	1	1.516	17%
SD	0.813	1	1.230	25%
AK	0.704			
DE	0.891			
VT	0.624			
WY	0.554			
UN				
XX				
TOT	308	365	1.600	14%

SO-7: Concentration of NCAA Division I Coaches by Games Coached

100+ GC				200+ GC					300+ GC					400+ GC				
State	Pop	#	Con	State	Pop	#	Con	%	State	Pop	#	Con	%	State	Pop	#	Con	%
IN	4.045	107	26.455	IN	4.045	66	16.318	61.7%	UT	1.042	10	9.600	45.5%	OK	2.300	14	6.086	50.0%
UT	1.042	22	21.121	UT	1.042	13	12.480	59.1%	IN	4.045	33	8.159	30.8%	IN	4.045	22	5.439	20.6%
KS	1.959	36	18.376	KY	2.999	31	10.335	60.8%	OK	2.300	17	7.391	60.7%	KS	1.959	10	5.104	27.8%
KY	2.999	51	17.004	WV	1.566	14	8.940	58.3%	KY	2.999	21	7.001	41.2%	KY	2.999	15	5.001	29.4%
WV	1.566	24	15.326	LA	2.797	25	8.937	71.4%	MS	2.070	12	5.797	42.9%	MS	2.070	10	4.831	35.7%
IA	2.448	35	14.299	OK	2.300	20	8.695	60.7%	WV	1.566	9	5.747	37.5%	UT	1.042	5	4.800	22.7%
PA	9.609	135	14.049	PA	9.609	82	8.534	60.7%	LA	2.797	16	5.720	45.7%	NY	13.631	55	4.035	30.7%
MS	2.070	28	13.526	NC	4.502	38	8.440	64.4%	NY	13.631	77	5.649	43.0%	PA	9.609	37	3.851	27.4%
NY	13.631	179	13.132	MS	2.070	17	8.212	60.7%	KS	1.959	11	5.615	30.6%	NC	4.502	17	3.776	28.8%
NC	4.502	59	13.105	KS	1.959	16	8.167	44.4%	IL	8.578	48	5.596	44.4%	MD	3.135	11	3.488	30.6%
VA	4.163	56	12.838	IL	8.578	67	7.811	62.0%	PA	9.609	50	5.203	37.0%	WI	3.529	12	3.400	46.2%
IL	8.578	108	12.591	CT	2.138	16	7.484	69.6%	MD	3.135	16.5	4.883	45.8%	LA	2.797	9	3.217	25.7%
LA	2.797	35	12.512	VA	4.163	32	7.446	57.1%	MO	4.014	18	4.484	66.7%	AR	1.885	6	3.184	42.9%
OH	7.793	97	12.448	OH	7.793	57	7.315	58.8%	WI	3.529	15	4.250	57.7%	IL	8.578	27	3.148	25.0%
OK	2.300	28	12.173	MD	3.135	23	6.976	63.9%	OH	7.793	33	4.235	34.0%	NJ	5.116	15	2.932	25.9%
NJ	5.116	58	11.338	NJ	5.116	33	6.451	56.9%	NC	4.502	19	4.220	32.2%	CT	2.138	6	2.806	26.1%
CT	2.138	23	10.758	IA	2.448	15	6.128	42.9%	NJ	5.116	21	4.105	36.2%	OR	2.300	6	2.608	46.2%
MD	3.135	36	10.464	WI	3.529	21	5.950	80.8%	VA	4.163	17.5	3.851	31.3%	WV	1.566	4	2.554	16.7%
MA	4.541	44	9.690	MA	4.541	26	5.726	59.1%	CT	2.138	8	3.742	34.8%	MO	4.014	10	2.491	37.0%
AL	2.999	26	8.668	AL	2.999	16	5.334	61.5%	IA	2.448	9	3.677	25.7%	OH	7.793	19	2.438	19.6%
MI	6.193	51	8.235	AR	1.885	10	5.306	71.4%	MA	4.541	16	3.524	36.4%	MA	4.541	10	2.202	22.7%
SC	2.390	18	7.531	MO	4.014	21	5.231	77.8%	AL	2.999	10	3.334	38.5%	TN	3.461	7	2.023	30.4%
AR	1.885	14	7.429	MI	6.193	27	4.360	52.9%	MI	6.193	20	3.229	39.2%	MI	6.193	12	1.938	23.5%
WI	3.529	26	7.367	WA	2.874	12	4.176	70.6%	OR	2.300	7	3.043	53.8%	CA	14.917	28	1.877	25.7%
CA	14.917	109	7.307	CA	14.917	61	4.089	56.0%	CA	14.917	40	2.681	36.7%	VA	4.163	8	1.797	14.3%
TX	10.273	72	7.008	TX	10.273	42	4.088	58.3%	CO	1.998	5	2.502	55.6%	WA	2.874	5	1.740	29.4%
MO	4.014	27	6.726	MN	3.140	11	3.503	68.8%	TN	3.461	8	2.312	34.8%	IA	2.448	4	1.634	11.4%
TN	3.461	23	6.646	CO	1.998	7	3.503	77.8%	MN	3.140	7	2.229	43.8%	MN	3.140	5	1.592	31.3%
WA	2.874	17	5.915	OR	2.300	8	3.478	61.5%	SC	2.390	5	2.092	27.8%	AL	2.999	4	1.334	15.4%
OR	2.300	13	5.652	TN	3.461	12	3.468	52.2%	WA	2.874	6	2.088	35.3%	SC	2.390	3	1.255	16.7%
GA	4.400	23	5.227	SC	2.390	8	3.347	44.4%	FL	6.169	12	1.945	52.2%	CO	1.998	2	1.001	22.2%
MN	3.140	16	5.096	GA	4.400	14	3.182	60.9%	TX	10.273	17	1.655	23.6%	FL	6.169	6	0.973	26.1%
CO	1.998	9	4.503	FL	6.169	15	2.432	65.2%	GA	4.400	7	1.591	30.4%	NE	2.152	2	0.929	33.3%
AZ	1.910	8	4.187	NE	2.152	5	2.324	83.3%	NE	2.152	2	0.929	33.3%	TX	10.273	9	0.876	12.5%
FL	6.169	23	3.728	AZ	1.910	3	1.570	37.5%	AZ	1.910	1	0.523	12.5%	GA	4.400	3	0.682	13.0%
NE	2.152	6	2.788											AZ	1.910	1	0.523	12.5%
DC	0.537	12	22.359	DC	0.537	6	11.180	50.0%	DC	0.537	5	9.316	41.7%	ID	0.687	4	5.823	36.4%
ID	0.687	11	16.012	MT	0.599	6	10.019	85.7%	ID	0.687	4	5.823	36.4%	DC	0.537	2	3.727	16.7%
WY	0.300	4	13.340	ND	0.565	5	8.848	83.3%	ND	0.565	3	5.309	50.0%	ND	0.565	2	3.539	33.3%
MT	0.599	7	11.689	RI	0.740	6	8.109	85.7%	MT	0.599	3	5.009	42.9%	NM	0.876	3	3.426	50.0%
ND	0.565	6	10.617	ID	0.687	5	7.278	45.5%	NM	0.876	4	4.568	66.7%	MT	0.599	2	3.340	28.6%
RI	0.740	7	9.461	WY	0.300	2	6.670	50.0%	WY	0.300	1	3.335	25.0%	WY	0.300	1	3.335	25.0%
ME	0.902	7	7.759	NM	0.876	5	5.710	83.3%	SD	0.613	2	3.262	50.0%	SD	0.613	1	1.631	25.0%
NH	0.676	5	7.393	ME	0.902	4	4.434	57.1%	RI	0.740	2	2.703	28.6%	ME	0.902	1	1.108	14.3%
NM	0.876	6	6.852	SD	0.613	2	3.262	50.0%	ME	0.902	2	2.217	28.6%	AK	0.262			
SD	0.613	4	6.524	NV	0.668	1	1.497	50.0%	NV	0.668	1	1.497	50.0%	DE	0.421			
NV	0.668	2	2.993	NH	0.676	1	1.479	20.0%	NH	0.676	1	1.479	20.0%	HI	0.624			
HI	0.624	1	1.602	AK	0.262				AK	0.262	0			NH	0.676			
AK	0.262			DE	0.421				DE	0.421	0			NV	0.668			
DE	0.421			HI	0.624				HI	0.624	0			RI	0.740			
VT	0.408			VT	0.408				VT	0.408	0			VT	0.408			
UN		21		UN		6		28.6%	UN		3		14.3%	UN				
XX		2		XX		1		50.0%	XX		1		50.0%	XX				
TOT		1725		TOT		1043		60.3%	TOT		662		38.2%	TOT		434		25.1%

SO-7: Concentration of NCAA Division I Coaches by Games Coached

500+ GC					600+ GC					700+ GC				
State	Pop	#	Con	%	State	Pop	#	Con	%	State	Pop	#	Con	%
OK	2.300	10	4.347	35.7%	KS	1.959	6	3.063	16.7%	OK	2.300	6	2.61	46.2%
IN	4.045	17	4.203	15.9%	OK	2.300	7	3.043	53.8%	KS	1.959	5	2.55	13.9%
MS	2.070	8	3.865	28.6%	UT	1.042	3	2.880	13.6%	IN	4.045	6	1.48	10.7%
UT	1.042	4	3.840	18.2%	MS	2.070	5	2.415	17.9%	MS	2.070	3	1.45	10.7%
KS	1.959	7	3.573	19.4%	IN	4.045	8	1.978	14.3%	NC	4.502	6	1.33	10.2%
KY	2.999	10	3.334	19.6%	NY	13.631	26	1.907	14.5%	NY	13.631	18	1.32	10.1%
WI	3.529	11	3.117	42.3%	MD	3.135	5.5	1.744	32.4%	MO	4.014	5	1.25	4.7%
NY	13.631	37	2.714	20.7%	KY	2.999	5	1.667	9.8%	WI	3.529	4	1.13	15.4%
AR	1.885	5	2.653	35.7%	IL	8.578	14	1.632	13.0%	MD	3.135	3.5	1.05	20.6%
LA	2.797	7	2.502	20.0%	PA	9.609	15	1.561	11.1%	OH	7.793	8	1.03	8.2%
PA	9.609	23	2.394	17.0%	NC	4.502	7	1.555	11.9%	KY	2.999	3	1	11.5%
OR	2.300	5	2.174	38.5%	OH	7.793	12	1.540	12.4%	UT	1.042	1	0.96	4.5%
NJ	5.116	11	2.150	19.0%	MO	4.014	6	1.495	5.6%	CT	2.138	2	0.94	8.7%
IL	8.578	18	2.098	16.7%	WI	3.529	5	1.417	19.2%	IL	8.578	8	0.93	7.4%
MD	3.135	7	2.093	19.4%	OR	2.300	3	1.304	10.7%	OR	2.300	2	0.87	7.1%
NC	4.502	9	1.999	15.3%	WV	1.566	2	1.277	8.3%	PA	9.609	8	0.83	5.9%
WV	1.566	3	1.916	12.5%	NJ	5.116	6	1.173	10.3%	NJ	5.116	4	0.78	6.9%
OH	7.793	14	1.797	14.4%	WA	2.874	3	1.044	11.5%	VA	4.163	3.5	0.77	13.0%
MO	4.014	7	1.744	25.9%	CT	2.138	2	0.935	8.7%	WA	2.874	2	0.7	3.9%
WA	2.874	5	1.740	29.4%	NE	2.152	2	0.929	33.3%	MA	4.541	3	0.66	6.8%
VA	4.163	7	1.541	12.5%	CA	14.917	13	0.871	11.9%	WV	1.566	1	0.64	4.2%
MI	6.193	9	1.453	17.6%	VA	4.163	3.5	0.770	13.0%	NE	2.152	1	0.46	16.7%
TN	3.461	5	1.445	21.7%	LA	2.797	2	0.715	5.7%	CA	14.917	6	0.4	5.5%
CT	2.138	3	1.403	13.0%	MA	4.541	3	0.661	6.8%	LA	2.797	1	0.36	2.9%
CA	14.917	19	1.274	17.4%	MI	6.193	4	0.646	7.8%	FL	6.169	2	0.32	8.7%
SC	2.390	3	1.255	16.7%	FL	6.169	3	0.486	13.0%	MN	3.140	1	0.32	6.3%
IA	2.448	3	1.226	8.6%	SC	2.390	1	0.418	5.6%	TX	10.273	2	0.19	2.8%
MA	4.541	5	1.101	11.4%	MN	3.140	1	0.318	6.3%	MI	6.193	1	0.16	2.0%
AL	2.999	3	1.000	11.5%	TN	3.461	1	0.289	4.3%	AL	2.999			
MN	3.140	3	0.955	18.8%	GA	4.400	1	0.227	4.3%	AR	1.885			
NE	2.152	2	0.929	33.3%	TX	10.273	2	0.195	2.8%	AZ	1.910			
FL	6.169	4	0.648	17.4%	AL	2.999	0	0.000	0.0%	CO	1.998			
TX	10.273	6	0.584	8.3%	AR	1.885	0	0.000	0.0%	GA	4.400			
AZ	1.910	1	0.523	12.5%	AZ	1.910	0	0.000	0.0%	IA	2.448			
CO	1.998	1	0.500	11.1%	CO	1.998	0	0.000	0.0%	SC	2.390			
GA	4.400	2	0.455	8.7%	IA	2.448	0	0.000	0.0%	TN	3.461			
DC	0.537	2	3.727	16.7%	ND	0.565	2	3.539	33.3%	ND	0.565	2	3.54	33.3%
ND	0.565	2	3.539	33.3%	WY	0.300	1	3.335	25.0%	NM	0.876	2	2.28	33.3%
WY	0.300	1	3.335	25.0%	ID	0.687	2	2.911	18.2%	DC	0.537	1	1.86	8.3%
ID	0.687	2	2.911	18.2%	NM	0.876	2	2.284	33.3%	ID	0.687	1	1.46	9.1%
NM	0.876	2	2.284	33.3%	DC	0.537	1	1.863	8.3%	AK	0.262			
MT	0.599	1	1.670	14.3%	AK	0.262				DE	0.421			
SD	0.613	1	1.631	25.0%	DE	0.421				HI	0.624			
AK	0.262				HI	0.624				ME	0.902			
DE	0.421				ME	0.902				MT	0.599			
HI	0.624				MT	0.599				NH	0.676			
ME	0.902				NH	0.676				NV	0.668			
NH	0.676				NV	0.668				RI	0.740			
NV	0.668				RI	0.740				SD	0.613			
RI	0.740				SD	0.613				VT	0.408			
VT	0.408				VT	0.408				WY	0.300			
UN					UN					UN				
XX					XX					XX				
TOT		303		17.6%	TOT		185		10.7%	TOT		122		7.1%

SO-7: Concentration of NCAA Division I Coaches by Games Coached

800+ GC

State	Pop	#	Con	%
KS	1.959	5	2.552	13.9%
OK	2.300	5	2.174	38.5%
IN	4.045	5	1.236	8.9%
MO	4.014	4	0.996	3.7%
UT	1.042	1	0.960	4.5%
CT	2.138	2	0.935	8.7%
OR	2.300	2	0.869	7.1%
IL	8.578	6	0.699	5.6%
MD	3.135	2.5	0.698	14.7%
KY	2.999	2	0.667	7.7%
NC	4.502	3	0.666	5.1%
NY	13.631	9	0.660	5.0%
OH	7.793	5	0.642	5.2%
WV	1.566	1	0.639	4.2%
NJ	5.116	3	0.586	5.2%
WI	3.529	2	0.567	7.7%
NE	2.152	1	0.465	16.7%
PA	9.609	4	0.416	3.0%
WA	2.874	1	0.348	2.0%
FL	6.169	2	0.324	8.7%
MN	3.140	1	0.318	6.3%
CA	14.917	4	0.268	3.7%
VA	4.163	1.5	0.257	5.6%
MA	4.541	1	0.220	2.3%
MI	6.193	1	0.161	2.0%
TX	10.273	1	0.097	1.4%
AL	2.999			
AR	1.885			
AZ	1.910			
CO	1.998			
GA	4.400			
IA	2.448			
LA	2.797			
MS	2.070			
SC	2.390			
TN	3.461			
DC	0.537	1	1.863	8.3%
ND	0.565	1	1.770	16.7%
NM	0.876	1	1.142	16.7%
AK	0.262			
DE	0.421			
HI	0.624			
ID	0.687			
ME	0.902			
MT	0.599			
NH	0.676			
NV	0.668			
RI	0.740			
SD	0.613			
VT	0.408			
WY	0.300			
UN				
XX				
TOT		78		4.5%

900+ GC

State	Pop	#	Con	%
KS	1.959	4	2.042	11.1%
OK	2.300	3	1.304	23.1%
UT	1.042	1	0.960	4.5%
MO	4.014	3	0.747	2.8%
IN	4.045	3	0.742	5.4%
KY	2.999	2	0.667	7.7%
NC	4.502	3	0.666	5.1%
WV	1.566	1	0.639	4.2%
OH	7.793	4	0.513	4.1%
CT	2.138	1	0.468	4.3%
NE	2.152	1	0.465	16.7%
OR	2.300	1	0.435	3.6%
NJ	5.116	2	0.391	3.4%
MD	3.135	1	0.349	5.9%
NY	13.631	4	0.293	2.2%
WI	3.529	1	0.283	3.8%
VA	4.163	1	0.257	3.7%
IL	8.578	2	0.233	1.9%
MA	4.541	1	0.220	2.3%
FL	6.169	1	0.162	4.3%
CA	14.917	2	0.134	1.8%
PA	9.609	1	0.104	0.7%
TX	10.273	1	0.097	1.4%
AL	2.999			
AR	1.885			
AZ	1.910			
CO	1.998			
GA	4.400			
IA	2.448			
LA	2.797			
MI	6.193			
MN	3.140			
MS	2.070			
SC	2.390			
TN	3.461			
WA	2.874			
ND	0.565	1	1.770	16.7%
NM	0.876	1	1.142	16.7%
AK	0.262			
DC	0.537			
DE	0.421			
HI	0.624			
ID	0.687			
ME	0.902			
MT	0.599			
NH	0.676			
NV	0.668			
RI	0.740			
SD	0.613			
VT	0.408			
WY	0.300			
UN				
XX				
TOT		46		2.7%

1000+ GC

State	Pop	#	Con	%
KS	1.959	4	2.042	11.1%
OK	2.300	2	0.869	15.4%
KY	2.999	2	0.667	3.9%
CT	2.138	1	0.468	4.3%
NC	4.502	2	0.444	3.4%
OR	2.300	1	0.435	3.6%
OH	7.793	3	0.385	3.1%
VA	4.163	1	0.257	3.7%
MO	4.014	1	0.249	0.9%
IN	4.045	1	0.247	1.8%
IL	8.578	2	0.233	1.9%
MA	4.541	1	0.220	2.3%
NJ	5.116	1	0.195	1.7%
FL	6.169	1	0.162	4.3%
NY	13.631	2	0.147	1.1%
CA	14.917	2	0.134	1.8%
AL	2.999			
AR	1.885			
AZ	1.910			
CO	1.998			
GA	4.400			
IA	2.448			
LA	2.797			
MD	3.135			
MI	6.193			
MN	3.140			
MS	2.070			
NE	2.152			
PA	9.609			
SC	2.390			
TN	3.461			
TX	10.273			
UT	1.042			
WA	2.874			
WI	3.529			
WV	1.566			
ND	0.565	1	1.770	
NM	0.876	1	1.142	16.7%
AK	0.262			
DC	0.537			
DE	0.421			
HI	0.624			
ID	0.687			
ME	0.902			
MT	0.599			
NH	0.676			
NV	0.668			
RI	0.740			
SD	0.613			
VT	0.408			
WY	0.300			
UN				
XX				
TOT		29		1.7%

SO-HOF: Concentration of Hall of Famers

All HOFers			
State	Pop (M)	#	Con
KS	2.332	13	5.575
IN	5.149	19	3.690
NY	17.230	56	3.250
NJ	6.860	19	2.769
PA	11.575	31	2.678
KY	3.509	8	2.280
NC	6.087	13	2.136
IL	10.867	23	2.117
OK	2.879	6	2.084
OR	2.452	5	2.039
UT	1.492	3	2.011
LA	3.679	7	1.903
MO	4.844	9	1.858
MN	4.005	7	1.748
MS	2.470	4	1.619
WV	1.873	3	1.602
MA	5.595	8	1.430
VA	5.248	7	1.334
AR	2.251	3	1.333
MI	8.346	11	1.318
OH	9.997	12	1.200
CA	22.620	25	1.105
CT	2.848	3	1.053
TN	4.479	4	0.893
WI	4.489	4	0.891
AL	3.754	3	0.799
NM	1.260	1	0.794
TX	14.515	10	0.689
NE	1.539	1	0.650
SC	3.099	2	0.645
MD	3.963	2	0.505
WA	4.098	2	0.488
GA	5.821	2	0.34
FL	9.560	3	0.31
DC	0.680	4	5.88
ND	0.640	2	3.12
NH	0.880	2	2.27
HI	0.893	1	1.12
RI	0.919	1	1.09
XX		32	
TOT		371	

Players			
State	Pop (M)	#	Con
IN	5.149	9	1.748
NY	17.230	30	1.741
KY	3.509	6	1.710
LA	3.679	6	1.631
AR	2.251	3	1.333
NC	6.087	8	1.314
KS	2.332	3	1.286
NJ	6.860	8	1.166
WV	1.873	2	1.068
OK	2.879	3	1.042
PA	11.575	12	1.037
MO	4.844	5	1.032
VA	5.248	5	0.953
MI	8.346	7	0.839
AL	3.754	3	0.799
CA	22.620	17	0.752
MN	4.005	3	0.749
IL	10.867	8	0.736
UT	1.492	1	0.670
SC	3.099	2	0.645
OH	9.997	5	0.500
WA	4.098	2	0.488
TN	4.479	2	0.447
TX	14.515	6	0.413
OR	2.452	1	0.408
MS	2.470	1	0.405
MA	5.595	2	0.357
CT	2.848	1	0.351
GA	5.821	2	0.344
MD	3.963	1	0.252
WI	4.489	1	0.223
FL	9.560	2	0.209
DC	0.680	2	2.94
XX		15	
TOT		184	

Coaches			
State	Pop (M)	#	Con
KS	2.332	6	2.573
MS	2.470	3	1.214
IN	5.149	6	1.165
OK	2.879	3	1.042
PA	11.575	12	1.037
OR	2.452	2	0.816
NM	1.260	1	0.794
NY	17.230	12	0.696
UT	1.492	1	0.670
NC	6.087	4	0.657
NE	1.539	1	0.650
MO	4.844	3	0.619
NJ	6.860	4	0.583
KY	3.509	2	0.570
IL	10.867	6	0.552
MN	4.005	2	0.499
WI	4.489	2	0.446
OH	9.997	4	0.400
MA	5.595	2	0.357
TX	14.515	4	0.276
LA	3.679	1	0.272
TN	4.479	1	0.223
CA	22.620	4	0.177
MI	8.346	1	0.120
MD	4.303	0.5	0.116
FL	9.560	1	0.105
VA	5.588	0.5	0.089
ND	0.640	2	3.123
DC	0.680	1	1.470
NH	0.880	1	1.136
XX		10	
TOT		103	

Contributors			
State	Pop (M)	#	Con
KS	2.332	3	1.286
OR	2.452	2	0.816
IN	5.149	4	0.777
IL	10.867	8	0.736
NJ	6.860	5	0.729
CT	2.848	2	0.702
UT	1.492	1	0.670
NY	17.230	10	0.580
MA	5.595	3	0.536
WV	1.873	1	0.534
MN	4.005	2	0.499
VA	5.248	2	0.381
PA	11.575	4	0.346
OH	9.997	3	0.300
MI	8.346	2	0.240
TN	4.479	1	0.223
WI	4.489	1	0.223
MO	4.844	1	0.206
NC	6.087	1	0.164
CA	22.620	3	0.133
NH	0.880	1	1.136
HI	0.893	1	1.120
RI	0.919	1	1.088
XX		7	
TOT		69	

Why Indiana is the Center of the Basketball World

SO-NBA PLAYERS: Career Stats for NBA Players from Indiana

Name	1st	Last	Yrs	GP	Min	Pts	Ast	Stl	Oreb	Dreb	Reb	Blk	TO	PF	FG%	FT%	3G%
Zachary Randolph	01/02	16/17	16	1058	33,127	17,467	1,883	772	3,132	6,527	9,659	313	2,156	2,497	47.17%	76.49%	25.39%
Shawn Kemp	89/90	02/03	14	1051	29,291	15,347	1,704	1,185	3,026	5,808	8,834	1,279	2,724	3,840	48.81%	74.14%	27.73%
Oscar Robertson*	60/61	73/74	14	1040	43,886	26,710	9,887	77	2,456	5,348	7,804	4		2,931	48.46%	83.77%	0.00%
Dick Barnett	59/60	73/74	14	971	28,937	15,358	2,729	1	877	1,935	2,812			2,514	45.62%	76.09%	0.00%
Rick Fox	91/92	03/04	13	930	23,722	8,966	2,649	967	996	2,521	3,517	355	1,611	2,739	44.98%	77.02%	34.89%
Tom Van Arsdale	65/66	76/77	12	929	28,682	14,232	2,085	230	1,135	2,807	3,942	16		2,922	43.13%	76.24%	
Dick Van Arsdale	65/66	76/77	12	921	31,771	15,079	3,060	264	1,150	2,657	3,807	44		2,575	46.42%	78.98%	
Larry Bird*	79/80	91/92	13	897	34,443	21,791	5,695	1,556	1,757	7,217	8,974	755	2,816	2,279	49.56%	88.57%	37.58%
Brad Miller	98/99	11/12	14	868	24,545	9,724	2,470	638	1,708	4,491	6,199	592	1,367	2,383	48.03%	80.38%	32.95%
Junior Bridgeman	75/76	86/87	12	849	21,257	11,517	2,066	685	910	2,085	2,995	220	1,169	1,969	47.54%	84.61%	24.39%
Calbert Cheaney	93/94	05/06	13	825	22,016	7,826	1,398	659	732	1,878	2,610	197	994	2,073	46.58%	69.10%	29.82%
Jon McGlocklin	65/66	75/76	11	792	20,930	9,169	2,280	102	567	1,361	1,928	13		1,370	48.95%	84.50%	
Mike Woodson	80/81	90/91	11	786	20,021	10,981	1,822	952	655	1,183	1,838	275	1,331	1,847	46.65%	81.26%	27.09%
Mike Conley Jr.	07/08	16/17	10	706	22,985	10,050	4,011	1,055	300	1,761	2,061	137	1,303	1,401	44.27%	81.48%	37.93%
Clyde Lovellette*	53/54	63/64	11	704	19,075	11,947	1,097		1,999	4,664	6,663			2,289	44.32%	75.74%	
Allen Leavell	79/80	88/89	10	700	16,248	6,684	3,339	929	294	870	1,164	120	1,324	1,489	44.99%	83.38%	23.38%
Glenn Robinson	94/95	04/05	11	688	25,343	14,232	1,879	826	1,027	3,160	4,187	389	2,147	1,847	45.93%	81.96%	34.01%
Kent Benson	77/78	87/88	11	680	15,719	6,168	1,203	605	1,216	2,665	3,881	586	1,069	1,935	49.35%	75.73%	20.59%
Courtney Lee	08/09	16/17	9	677	18,855	6,609	1,124	690	318	1,499	1,817	187	653	1,165	45.08%	84.83%	38.64%
Terry Dischinger	62/63	72/73	9	652	17,841	9,012	1,151	0	1,116	2,530	3,646			2,055	50.57%	75.79%	
Alan Henderson	95/96	06/07	12	652	13,775	5,094	397	362	1,425	1,824	3,249	297	717	1,436	46.88%	63.95%	19.23%
Don Buse	76/77	84/85	9	648	17,070	4,485	2,920	1,160	373	1,134	1,507	97	601	967	44.19%	77.96%	33.33%
John Mengelt	71/72	80/81	10	636	12,788	6,218	1,329	324	309	912	1,221	28	280	1,284	47.91%	80.91%	
Jared Jeffries	02/03	12/13	11	628	13,566	3,003	797	434	1,166	1,396	2,562	323	673	1,527	42.63%	58.30%	25.00%
Larry Steele	71/72	79/80	9	610	14,777	5,009	1,719	846	568	1,213	1,781	96	195	1,832	48.33%	79.56%	
Scott Skiles	86/87	95/96	10	600	16,789	6,652	3,881	500	275	1,251	1,526	29	1,497	1,343	43.54%	88.91%	37.94%
George Hill	08/09	16/17	9	599	17,357	7,039	2,003	555	333	1,591	1,924	176	789	1,289	45.28%	80.16%	37.96%
Jeff Teague	09/10	16/17	8	599	16,175	7,545	3,310	713	192	1,252	1,444	205	1,349	1,119	44.69%	84.44%	35.52%
Jerry Sichting	80/81	89/90	10	598	12,732	4,141	1,962	439	196	621	817	19	657	940	50.67%	85.69%	27.12%
Jim Davis	67/68	74/75	8	597	10,027	3,997	739	89	957	2,152	3,109	66		1,463	46.13%	67.44%	
Walter McCarty	96/97	05/06	10	593	10,372	3,056	670	380	410	1,144	1,554	173	518	1,211	39.20%	69.80%	34.60%
Bonzi Wells	98/99	07/08	10	591	15,138	7,147	1,249	769	800	1,937	2,737	192	1,215	1,526	46.05%	69.68%	32.65%
Kyle Macy	80/81	86/87	7	551	14,246	5,259	2,198	631	311	903	1,214	49	712	1,081	50.13%	87.33%	33.80%
Randy Wittman	83/84	91/92	9	543	11,594	4,034	1,201	257	187	573	760	65	441	559	50.14%	75.25%	32.08%
Bob Wilkerson	76/77	82/83	7	536	14,883	5,424	1,835	671	587	1,649	2,236	141	1,156	1,310	42.46%	75.15%	16.67%
George McGinnis*	75/76	81/82	7	528	16,194	9,090	1,985	923	1,601	3,576	5,177	236	1,291	1,984	44.75%	65.07%	8.00%
Gordon Hayward	10/11	16/17	7	516	16,164	8,077	1,762	527	377	1,772	2,149	215	1,059	923	44.40%	82.04%	36.79%
Winston Garland	87/88	94/95	7	511	13,388	4,799	2,421	674	413	1,020	1,433	80	975	1,251	43.02%	82.98%	28.08%
Jim Price	72/73	78/79	7	510	12,815	5,088	1,886	724	425	1,141	1,566	126	275	1,369	44.37%	81.53%	
Eric Gordon	08/09	16/17	9	492	16,471	8,151	1,559	491	224	1,027	1,251	160	1,050	985	43.06%	81.65%	38.03%
Eric Montross	94/95	01/02	8	465	8,481	2,071	207	122	716	1,443	2,159	275	405	1,270	48.98%	47.85%	0.00%
Josh McRoberts	07/08	16/17	10	431	8,266	2,333	901	222	468	1,218	1,686	194	381	815	46.37%	70.55%	34.09%
Bob Leonard	56/57	62/63	7	426	11,632	4,204	1,427		372	845	1,217			915	34.90%	74.47%	
John Barnhill	62/63	68/69	7	426	10,054	3,648	1,205	0	372	821	1,193			751	41.59%	65.11%	
Chuck Noble	55/56	61/62	7	411	9,212	3,276	1,344		341	734	1,075			1,128	34.59%	73.11%	
E'Twaun Moore	11/12	16/17	6	380	7,106	2,489	648	229	145	522	667	95	310	540	43.52%	74.90%	36.92%
Leo Barnhorst	49/50	53/54	5	344	7,279	3,232	1,116		477	1,029	1,506			1,033	36.76%	66.50%	
Tyler Zeller	12/13	16/17	5	340	6,048	2,384	316	88	513	974	1,487	203	297	751	49.95%	76.92%	0.00%
Tom Abernethy	76/77	80/81	5	319	5,434	1,779	384	185	374	637	1,011	60	129	525	49.18%	74.72%	0.00%
Paul Hoffman	47/48	54/55	6	317	5,130	3,234	911		345	784	1,129			1,138	33.96%	67.56%	
Lee Nailon	00/01	05/06	6	305	5,817	2,622	298	133	379	556	935	53	320	596	47.38%	78.63%	11.11%
Rodney Carney	06/07	10/11	5	299	4,605	1,778	132	159	164	425	589	99	157	420	42.21%	70.37%	33.84%
Vince Boryla	49/50	53/54	5	285	5,162	3,187	610		273	558	831			922	37.09%	81.63%	
Cody Zeller	13/14	16/17	4	279	6,402	2,239	362	193	488	1,087	1,575	211	282	719	49.97%	73.36%	15.38%
Bob Donham	50/51	53/54	4	273	4,866	1,818	706		328	743	1,071			850	48.01%	50.67%	
Gene Tormohlen	62/63	69/70	6	271	3,223	1,191	257	0	360	762	1,122			551	41.10%	57.91%	
Tellis Frank	87/88	93/94	5	264	4,703	1,710	276	158	363	659	1,022	95	326	795	43.89%	74.10%	0.00%

Why Indiana is the Center of the Basketball World

Name	1st	Last	Yrs	GP	Min	Pts	Ast	Stl	Oreb	Dreb	Reb	Blk	TO	PF	FG%	FT%	3G%
Ray Tolbert	81/82	88/89	5	261	2,789	928	135	71	221	388	609	101	210	418	49.50%	54.40%	0.00%
Johnny Logan	46/47	50/51	5	257		3,196	783	0	41	93	134			740	31.17%	76.66%	
Bryce Drew	98/99	03/04	6	243	3,971	1,081	524	123	56	239	295	10	209	291	38.23%	83.04%	37.13%
Lou Dampier*	76/77	78/79	3	232	4,431	1,553	643	171	61	200	261	36	134	219	48.80%	74.78%	
Bill Dinwiddie	67/68	71/72	4	220	2,760	974	129	0	220	500	720			381	36.89%	61.03%	
Henry James	90/91	97/98	7	212	2,703	1,292	87	48	106	212	318	18	134	306	41.44%	80.99%	37.81%
Dick Farley	54/55	58/59	3	211	3,822	1,378	386		161	366	527			429	38.42%	70.03%	
Greg Graham	93/94	97/98	5	207	2,530	938	201	128	59	160	219	12	179	213	40.71%	77.47%	28.99%
Larry Demic	79/80	81/82	3	206	3,192	976	106	72	338	467	805	49	252	524	45.90%	57.96%	0.00%
David Johnson	49/50	52/53	4	204	2,295	1,705	569		147	351	498			703	32.69%	73.96%	
Bill Tosheff	51/52	53/54	3	203	6,339	1,859	661		186	422	608			654	31.51%	79.33%	
Gary Harris	14/15	16/17	3	188	4,940	1,971	340	207	123	339	462	33	212	306	46.02%	78.98%	35.57%
Tom Kron	66/67	68/69	3	184	3,139	1,193	518	0	194	409	603			445	38.86%	75.32%	
Steve Alford	87/88	90/91	4	169	1,641	744	176	85	25	119	144	10	89	113	45.90%	86.99%	32.41%
Willie McCarter	69/70	71/72	3	155	2,842	1,090	304	0	73	175	248			281	40.23%	65.63%	
Ray McCallum	13/14	15/16	3	154	2,808	920	368	79	78	228	306	27	148	190	40.83%	71.13%	33.49%
Paul Armstrong	48/49	50/51	3	153		1,040	358		27	62	89			456	29.51%	69.20%	
Steve Green	76/77	78/79	3	153	1,632	705	97	71	132	168	300	17	40	263	43.84%	70.44%	
Trey Lyles	15/16	16/17	2	151	2,540	928	128	52	107	427	534	38	129	211	40.00%	70.81%	34.34%
Glenn Robinson, Jr	14/15	16/17	3	149	2,196	663	84	64	84	269	353	30	66	99	44.78%	69.78%	37.57%
Cliff Barker	49/50	51/52	3	149	494	557	294		58	123	181			253	31.55%	66.24%	
Mike Flynn	76/77	77/78	2	144	2,279	896	321	98	123	181	304	16	75	158	44.05%	65.27%	
Bobby Wilson	74/75	77/78	4	143	1,498	792	110	52	59	108	167	4	6	185	42.65%	77.27%	
Herm Schaefer	48/49	49/50	2	123		932	388							225	37.92%	82.80%	
Mike Price	70/71	72/73	3	123	1,067	397	90	0	48	109	157			173	40.25%	77.17%	
Sean May	05/06	09/10	4	119	1,868	821	115	53	155	326	481	47	134	236	45.76%	74.56%	23.08%
Ralph O'Brien	51/52	52/53	2	119	2,335	848	180		65	127	192			189	36.04%	82.99%	
Ron Reed	65/66	66/67	2	118	2,245	951	173	0	242	520	762			278	36.39%	57.08%	
John Laskowski	75/76	76/77	2	118	2,132	832	99	88	68	214	282	12		112	39.80%	76.00%	
Bill Roberts	48/49	49/50	2	117		404	65							203	33.95%	70.59%	
Dave Minor	51/52	52/53	2	116	3,168	877	288		155	372	527			372	35.99%	75.38%	
Leo Klier	48/49	49/50	2	113		802	177							301	27.98%	72.78%	
Duane Klueh	49/50	50/51	2	113		924	173		54	129	183			254	36.24%	71.92%	
Mel Payton	51/52	52/53	2	111	1,895	595	126		128	268	396			186	36.32%	74.60%	
Greg Oden	08/09	13/14	3	105	2,028	840	51	40	256	400	656	130	138	374	57.43%	65.81%	0.00%
Milt Schoon	46/47	49/50	2	103		616	96							265	34.16%	60.53%	
Wallace Bryant	83/84	85/86	3	102	1,395	323	112	35	128	246	374	40	71	196	40.73%	57.29%	0.00%
Brian Evans	96/97	98/99	3	102	1,097	375	77	35	56	108	164	18	42	115	38.10%	81.97%	34.26%
Eddie Ehlers	47/48	48/49	2	99		800	177							211	28.60%	61.79%	
Robbie Hummel	13/14	14/15	2	98	1,397	379	50	32	66	200	266	11	28	143	41.83%	86.67%	34.29%
Marcus Teague	12/13	13/14	2	88	835	206	121	19	4	80	84	12	74	93	34.91%	68.63%	21.95%
Ted Luckenbill	61/62	62/63	2	87	597	196	35	0	54	112	166			101	36.70%	60.42%	
Steve Hamilton	58/59	59/60	2	82	1,094	368	43		87	191	278			183	37.20%	69.70%	
Ron Bonham	64/65	65/66	2	76	681	478	30	0	36	77	113			62	39.11%	83.24%	
Ed Stanczak	49/50	50/51	2	74		578	73		10	24	34			172	33.73%	76.04%	
Dave Schellhase	66/67	67/68	2	73	513	208	60	0	23	53	76			70	34.94%	56.67%	
Joe Cooke	70/71	70/71	1	73	725	316	93	0	35	79	114			135	39.30%	81.36%	
Luke Harangody	10/11	11/12	2	70	871	253	36	21	60	136	196	20	20	97	37.64%	73.68%	24.14%
John Janisch	46/47	47/48	2	70		734	51							137	28.75%	65.42%	
Jack Turner	54/55	54/55	1	65	922	282	77		51	103	154			76	36.04%	78.95%	
Milo Komenich	49/50	49/50	1	64		634	124							246	28.34%	58.40%	
Craig Neal	88/89	90/91	2	63	625	158	155	28	9	36	45	4	73	96	37.34%	60.00%	30.23%
Bob Lochmueller	52/53	52/53	1	62	802	232	47		51	111	162			143	32.24%	60.66%	
Chris Hunter	09/10	09/10	1	60	783	270	37	13	56	111	167	35	30	132	50.23%	75.36%	
George Sobek	49/50	49/50	1	60		346	95							158	37.85%	76.10%	
Bob Dille	46/47	46/47	1	57		296	40							92	19.72%	66.67%	
Andre Owens	05/06	07/08	2	54	601	192	55	18	24	44	68	3	37	62	36.81%	71.15%	37.50%
Harold Brown	46/47	46/47	1	54		264	39							122	24.80%	63.25%	

Name	1st	Last	Yrs	GP	Min	Pts	Ast	Stl	Oreb	Dreb	Reb	Blk	TO	PF	FG%	FT%	3G%
Ward Williams	48/49	48/49	1	53		215	82							158	23.74%	75.00%	
Carl Shaeffer	49/50	50/51	2	53		165	46		3	7	10			118	35.71%	58.33%	
McGary Mitch	14/15	15/16	2	52	557	227	17	17	57	126	183	18	38	82	52.66%	58.00%	0.00%
Wayne Radford	78/79	78/79	1	52	649	202	57	30	25	43	68	1	45	61	47.43%	80.00%	
Ray Ragelis	51/52	51/52	1	51	337	68	31		23	53	76			62	26.04%	62.07%	
Monte Towe	76/77	76/77	1	51	409	130	87	16	8	26	34	0		61	40.58%	72.00%	
Forest Weber	46/47	46/47	1	50		173	4							111	29.21%	69.62%	
Earl Gardner	48/49	48/49	1	50		89	19							50	37.62%	46.43%	
Scott Haffner	89/90	90/91	2	50	609	213	89	16	9	46	55	3	37	57	40.34%	66.67%	13.04%
Ralph Hamilton	48/49	48/49	1	48		289	83							67	25.50%	67.03%	
Bob Evans	49/50	49/50	1	47		142	55							99	28.00%	68.18%	
Dick Dickey	51/52	51/52	1	45	440	127	50		24	57	81			79	29.41%	68.12%	
Richard Atha	55/56	57/58	2	43	448	137	51		20	46	66			63	39.26%	79.49%	
Bob Royer	49/50	49/50	1	42		197	85							72	33.77%	70.69%	
Nick Mantis	59/60	62/63	2	42	755	236	92	0	28	63	91			102	36.75%	54.90%	
R.J. Hunter	15/16	16/17	2	39	324	97	13	14	2	36	38	4	11	29	36.36%	85.71%	30.16%
Yogi Ferrell	16/17	16/17	1	39	1,197	462	172	42	20	91	111	9	70	90	40.61%	83.15%	38.64%
Sam Ranzino	51/52	51/52	1	39	234	86	25		12	27	39			63	33.33%	70.27%	
George Pearcy	46/47	46/47	1	37		94	13							68	23.85%	72.73%	
Frank Radovich	61/62	61/62	1	37	175	87	4	0	16	35	51			27	39.78%	50.00%	
JaJuan Johnson	11/12	11/12	1	36	298	114	6	5	20	38	58	14	14	25	44.63%	66.67%	0.00%
William Bell	59/60	60/61	2	36	494	183	56	0	28	66	94			66	37.93%	63.04%	
Jim Riffey	50/51	50/51	1	35		150	16		20	41	61			54	35.14%	76.92%	
Rod Freeman	73/74	73/74	1	35	265	106	14	12	22	32	54	1		42	37.86%	68.29%	
Ron Horn	61/62	62/63	2	31	314	77	11	0	24	53	77			50	29.79%	67.74%	
Porter Meriwether	62/63	62/63	1	31	268	119	43	0	9	20	29			19	39.34%	69.70%	
Chet Aubuchon	46/47	46/47	1	30		65	20							46	25.27%	54.29%	
Walter Jordan	80/81	80/81	1	30	207	68	11	11	23	19	42	5	17	35	38.67%	73.53%	0.00%
Henry Pearcy	46/47	46/47	1	29		73	7							20	22.22%	73.53%	
Harold Johnson	46/47	46/47	1	27		15	11							13	20.00%	50.00%	
Steve Downing	73/74	74/75	2	27	146	64	11	5	14	27	41	0		33	31.82%	55.00%	
Jim Grandholm	90/91	90/91	1	26	168	79	8	2	20	30	50	8	11	33	40.26%	81.82%	52.94%
Frank Kendrick	74/75	74/75	1	24	121	80	6	11	19	17	36	3		46	25.55%	72.55%	
Charley Shipp	49/50	49/50	1	23		107	46							21	40.48%	45.00%	50.00%
A.J. Hammons	16/17	16/17	1	22	163	48	4	1	8	28	36	13	10	5	34.62%	0.00%	20.00%
Luke Zeller	12/13	12/13	1	16	58	19	3	0	1	9	10	0	0	30	24.24%	47.37%	
Dale Hamilton	49/50	49/50	1	14		25	17							34	23.61%	71.43%	
Gene Ollrich	49/50	49/50	1	14		44	24							5	25.00%	50.00%	0.00%
Dave Magley	82/83	82/83	1	14	56	12	2	2	2	8	10	0	2	15	29.09%	86.84%	25.00%
Tony Harris	90/91	94/95	3	14	147	68	8	5	3	8	11	0	10	12	39.62%	50.00%	100.00%
Jerome Harmon	94/95	94/95	1	10	158	46	12	9	9	14	23	0	7	12	23.81%	33.33%	
Dick Wehr	48/49	48/49	1	9		12	3							11	25.81%	57.14%	
Jay Miller	67/68	67/68	1	8	52	20	1	0	2	5	7			9	55.56%	57.14%	
Don Bielke	55/56	55/56	1	7	38	14	1		3	6	9			2	40.00%	100.00%	0.00%
Branden Dawson	15/16	15/16	1	6	29	5	0	0	2	2	4	1	0	10	35.29%	85.71%	
John Hazen	48/49	48/49	1	6		18	3							6	0.00%	83.33%	0.00%
Roger Burkman	81/82	81/82	1	6	30	5	5	6	2	4	6	2	3	6	0.00%	83.33%	0.00%
Demetrius Jackson	16/17	16/17	1	5	17	10	3	0	2	2	4	0	0	0	75.00%	50.00%	100.00%
Darrell Elston	76/77	76/77	1	5	40	5	2	1	1	5	6	0		6	14.29%	50.00%	
Jack Parkinson	49/50	49/50	1	4		3	2							3	8.33%	100.00%	
Jay Edwards	89/90	89/90	1	4	26	7	4	1	1	1	2	0	1	4	42.86%	33.33%	0.00%
Rob Rensberger	46/47	46/47	1	3		0	0							4	0.00%	0.00%	
Marv Winkler	70/71	70/71	1	3	14	8	2	0	1	3	4			3	30.00%	100.00%	
Dexter Shouse	89/90	89/90	1	3	18	0	2	1	0	0	0	1	2	2	0.00%	0.00%	0.00%
Jim Springer	48/49	48/49	1	2		1	0							0	0.00%	100.00%	
Carl McNulty	54/55	54/55	1	1	14	2	0		0	0	0			1	16.67%	0.00%	

SO-AA: All-Americans from Indiana

Player	College	Year (Team)		
Larry Teeple	Purdue	1913 (1)		
Elmer Oliphant	Purdue	1914 (1)		
Elmer Oliphant	Army	1915 (1)		
Tony Hinkle	Chicago	1919 (1)	1920 (1)	
Donald White	Purdue	1921 (1)		
Everett Dean	Indiana	1921 (1)		
Ray Miller	Purdue	1922 (1)		
Noble Kizer	Notre Dame	1925 (1)		
George Spradling	Purdue	1926 (1)		
Strecth Murphy	Purdue	1928 (1)	1929 (1)	1930 (1)
John Wooden	Purdue	1930 (1)	1931 (1)	1932 (1)
Branch McCracken	Indiana	1930 (1)		
Norman Cotton	Purdue	1934 (1)		
Leroy Edwards	Kentucky	1935 (1)		
Paul Nowak	Notre Dame	1936 (1)	1937 (1)	1938 (1)
Robert Kessler	Purdue	1936 (1)		
Vern Huffman	Indiana	1936 (1)		
Jewell Young	Purdue	1937 (1)	1938 (1)	
Ernie Andres	Indiana	1939 (1)		
Ralph Vaughn	USC	1940 (1)		
Marv Huffman	Indiana	1940 (2)		
Gus Doerner	Evansville	1942 (2)		
Robert Rensberger	Notre Dame	1943 (2)		
Leo Klier	Notre Dame	1944 (1)		
Bob Dille	Valparaiso	1944 (2)		
Leo Klier	Notre Dame	1946 (1)		
Jack Parkinson	Kentucky	1946 (2)		
Ralph Hamilton	Indiana	1947 (1)		
Dick Dickey	NC State	1948 (3)		
Vince Boryla	Denver	1949 (1)		
Sam Ranzino	NC State	1950 (2)	1951 (1)	
Dick Dickey	NC State	1950 (2)		
Clyde Lovellette	Kansas	1950 (3)	1951 (1)	1952 (1)
Bill Garrett	Indiana	1951 (2)		
Don Schlundt	Indiana	1953 (2)	1954 (1)	1955 (2)
Slick Leonard	Indiana	1953 (3)	1954 (2)	
Oscar Robertson	Cincinnati	1958 (1)	1959 (1)	1960 (1)
Roger Kaiser	Georgia Tech	1960 (2)	1961 (1)	
Terry Dischinger	Purdue	1960 (2)	1961 (1)	1962 (1)

Why Indiana is the Center of the Basketball World

Player	College	Year (Team)		
Dick Hickox	Miami	1960 (3)		
Jimmy Rayl	Indiana	1962 (3)	1963 (3)	
Ron Bonham	Cincinnati	1963 (1)	1964 (2)	
Dave Schellhase	Purdue	1965 (2)	1966 (2)	
Louie Dampier	Kentucky	1966 (3)	1967 (3)	
Mike Warren	UCLA	1968 (3)		
Rick Mount	Purdue	1968 (3)	1969 (1)	1970 (1)
George McGinnis	Indiana	1971 (3)		
Jim Price	Louisville	1972 (2)		
Kent Benson	Indiana	1976 (1)	1977 (1)	
Larry Bird	Indiana State	1978 (1)	1979 (1)	
Kyle Macy	Kansas	1980 (1)		
Steve Alford	Indiana	1986 (1)	1987 (1)	
Scott Skiles	Michigan State	1986 (2)		
Jay Edwards	Indiana	1989 (2)		
Calbert Cheaney	Indiana	1991 (3)	1992 (3)	1993 (1)
Glenn Robinson	Purdue	1993 (2)	1994 (1)	
Eric Montross	North Carolina	1993 (2)	1994 (2)	
Damon Bailey	Indiana	1994 (3)		
Brian Evans	Indiana	1996 (3)		
Bonzie Wells	Ball State	1998 (3)		
Lee Nailon	TCU	1998 (3)		
Jared Jeffries	Indiana	2002 (2)		
Jason Gardner	Arizona	2002 (3)	2003 (2)	
Sean May	North Carolina	2005 (2)		
Rodney Carney	Memphis	2006 (2)		
Greg Oden	Ohio State	2007 (1)		
Luke Harangody	Notre Dame	2008 (2)	2009 (2)	2010 (3)
Eric Gordon	Indiana	2008 (3)		
JaJuan Johnson	Purdue	2011 (1)		
Tyler Zeller	North Carolina	2012 (2)		
Cody Zeller	Indiana	2013 (2)		
Deshaun Thomas	Ohio State	2013 (3)		
Yogi Ferrell	Indiana	2016 (3)		
Caleb Swanigan	Purdue	2017 (1)		

SO-NBA COACHES: Career Stats for NBA Coaches from Indiana

Name	Regular Season									Playoffs							
	1st Season	Latest Season	# Seasons	GC	Wins	Losses	Win%	# Win Sea	% Win Seasons	# Playoffs	% Playoff	GC	Wins	Losses	Win%	Finalist	Champ
Glenn Curtis	46/47	46/47	1	34	12	22	35%	0	0%								
Philip Sachs	46/47	46/47	1	26	8	18	31%	0	0%								
Carl Bennett	48/49	48/49	1	6	0	6	0%	0	0%								
Burl Friddle	48/49	48/49	1	43	14	29	33%	0	0%								
Curly Armstrong	48/49	48/49	1	54	22	32	41%	0	0%								
Murray Mendenhall	49/50	50/51	2	136	72	64	53%	1	50%	2	100%	7	3	4	43%		
Cliff Barker	49/50	50/51	2	120	63	57	53%	1	50%	1	50%	6	3	3	50%		
Ike Duffey	49/50	49/50	1	3	1	2	33%	0	0%								
Charley Shipp	49/50	49/50	1	35	8	27	23%	0	0%								
Doxie Moore	49/50	51/52	2	92	32	60	35%	1	50%	1	50%	8	4	4	50%		
John Logan	50/51	50/51	1	3	2	1	67%	1	100%								
Herm Schaefer	51/52	52/53	2	137	62	75	45%	1	50%	2	100%	4	0	4	0%		
Vince Boryla	55/56	57/58	3	165	80	85	48%	1	33%								
Bob Leonard	62/63	79/80	6	450	186	264	41%	0	0%								
Terry Dischinger	71/72	71/72	1	2	2	0	100%	1	100%								
John MacLeod	73/74	90/91	18	1364	707	657	52%	9	50%	11	61%	101	47	54	47%	1	
Gene Tormohlen	75/76	75/76	1	8	1	7	13%	0	0%								
Tates Locke	76/77	76/77	1	46	16	30	35%	0	0%								
Del Harris	79/80	98/99	14	1013	556	457	55%	11	79%	11	79%	88	38	50	43%	1	
Jerry Reynolds	86/87	89/90	4	170	56	114	33%	0	0%								
Dick VanArsdale	86/87	86/87	1	26	14	12	54%	1	100%								
Frank Hamblen	91/92	04/05	2	104	33	71	32%	0	0%								
Gregg Popovich	96/97	16/17	21	1656	1150	506	69%	20	95%	20	95%	272	166	106	61%	6	5
Larry Bird*	97/98	99/00	3	214	147	67	69%	3	100%	3	100%	52	32	20	62%	1	
Randy Wittman	99/00	15/16	10	684	278	406	41%	3	30%	2	20%	23	12	11	52%		
Scott Skiles	99/00	12/13	13	876	443	433	51%	7	54%	6	46%	42	18	24	43%		
Terry Stotts	02/03	16/17	9	693	338	355	49%	4	44%	5	56%	36	12	24	33%		
Mike Woodson	04/05	13/14	9	680	315	365	46%	4	44%	5	56%	46	18	28	39%		
Brad Stevens	13/14	16/17	4	246	118	128	48%	1	25%	3	75%	28	11	17	39%		

SO-NCAA COACHES: Career Stats for NCAA Coaches from Indiana

Coach	1st Season	Latest Season	# Years	RS Win	RS Loss	RS GC	RS Win%	1st Tourn	Latest Tourn	# Tourn	Tourn GC	Tourn Win	Tourn Loss	Tourn Win%	Finals	Champ	TOT GC	TOT Win	TOT Loss	TOT Win%
Steve Alford	1994/95	2016/17	22	732	481	1213	60.35%	1999	2017	10	21	11	10	52.38%			1234	743	491	60.21%
Tony Hinkle*	1926/27	1969/70	41	558	394	952	58.61%	1962	1962	1	3	2	1	66.67%			955	560	395	58.64%
Norm Sloan	1956/57	1988/89	33	558	359	917	60.85%	1970	1989	6	13	8	5	61.54%	1	1	930	566	364	60.86%
John Wooden*	1946/47	1974/75	29	664	162	826	80.39%	1950	1975	16	56	47	9	83.93%	10	10	882	711	171	80.61%
Arad McCutchan*	1946/47	1976/77	31	513	313	826	62.11%										826	513	313	62.11%
Matt Painter	2005/06	2016/17	13	437	290	727	60.11%	2004	2017	10	20	10	10	50.00%			747	447	300	59.84%
Gary Colson	1968/69	1994/95	24	375	316	691	54.27%	1976	1979	2	4	2	2	50.00%			695	377	318	54.24%
Donald White	1923/24	1962/63	33	301	332	633	47.55%										633	301	332	47.55%
Everett Dean*	1921/22	1950/51	28	375	217	592	63.34%	1942	1942	1	3	3	0	100.00%	1	1	595	378	217	63.53%
Ray McCallum	1993/94	2015/16	19	300	281	581	51.64%	1995	2012	3	3	0	3	0.00%			584	300	284	51.37%
Branch McCracken*	1938/39	1964/65	24	364	174	538	67.66%	1940	1958	4	11	9	2	81.82%	2	2	549	373	176	67.94%
Everett Case*	1946/47	1964/65	19	377	134	511	73.78%	1950	1956	5	12	6	6	50.00%			523	383	140	73.23%
"Piggy" Lambert*	1916/17	1945/46	29	371	152	523	70.94%										523	371	152	70.94%
Forddy Anderson	1946/47	1964/65	19	299	203	502	59.56%	1950	1959	4	13	9	4	69.23%	2		515	308	207	59.81%
Tates Locke	1963/64	1993/94	19	244	264	508	48.03%	1969	1979	2	4	1	3	25.00%			512	245	267	47.85%
Barry Collier	1989/90	2005/06	17	285	223	508	56.10%	1997	2000	3	3	0	3	0.00%			511	285	226	55.77%
Scott Drew	2002/03	2016/17	15	299	191	490	61.02%	2008	2017	7	17	10	7	58.82%			507	309	198	60.95%
Brad Brownell	2002/03	2016/17	15	291	188	479	60.75%	2003	2011	4	5	1	4	20.00%			484	292	192	60.33%
Ron Greene	1966/67	1988/89	16	226	212	438	51.60%										438	226	212	51.60%
Steve Yoder	1977/78	1991/92	15	205	227	432	47.45%	1981	1981	1	1	0	1	0.00%			433	205	228	47.34%
Clifford Wells*	1945/46	1962/63	18	254	171	425	59.76%										425	254	171	59.76%
Ritchie McKay	1998/99	2016/17	13	214	190	404	52.97%	2005	2005	1	1	0	1	0.00%			405	214	191	52.84%
John MacLeod	1967/68	1998/99	14	196	193	389	50.39%										389	196	193	50.39%
Blair Gullion	1935/36	1958/59	18	219	157	376	58.24%										376	219	157	58.24%
Roy Danforth	1968/69	1980/81	13	193	161	354	54.52%	1973	1976	4	9	5	4	55.56%			363	198	165	54.55%
Gordon Stauffer	1971/72	1989/90	13	153	192	345	44.35%										345	153	192	44.35%
Ray Eddy	1950/51	1964/65	15	176	164	340	51.76%										340	176	164	51.76%
Eddie Cameron	1924/25	1941/42	15	234	104	338	69.23%										338	234	104	69.23%
Joe Sexson	1977/78	1988/89	12	143	188	331	43.20%										331	143	188	43.20%
Tim Jankovich	1993/94	2016/17	11	196	126	322	60.87%	2017	2017	1	1	0	1	0.00%			323	196	127	60.68%
John Groce	2008/09	2016/17	9	180	131	311	57.88%	2012	2013	2	5	3	2	60.00%			316	183	133	57.91%
Les Wothke	1979/80	1989/90	11	134	176	310	43.23%										310	134	176	43.23%
Dan Dakich	1997/98	2007/08	11	159	144	303	52.48%										303	159	144	52.48%
Vic Bubas	1959/60	1968/69	10	213	67	280	76.07%	1960	1966	4	15	11	4	73.33%	1		295	224	71	75.93%
Todd Lickliter	2001/02	2009/10	9	169	119	288	58.68%	2003	2007	2	6	4	2	66.67%			294	173	121	58.84%
Bret Campbell	1999/00	2008/09	10	125	168	293	42.66%										293	125	168	42.66%
Bill Hodges	1978/79	1996/97	10	129	155	284	45.42%	1979	1979	1	5	4	1	80.00%	1		289	133	156	46.02%
Steve Steinwedel	1985/86	1994/95	10	163	121	284	57.39%	1992	1993	2	2	0	2	0.00%			286	163	123	56.99%
Mike Newell	1984/85	1992/93	9	175	104	279	62.72%	1986	1990	3	4	1	3	25.00%			283	176	107	62.19%
Emmet Lowery	1947/48	1958/59	12	169	110	279	60.57%										279	169	110	60.57%
Sean Woods	2008/09	2016/17	9	127	150	277	45.85%	2012	2012	1	1	0	1	0.00%			278	127	151	45.68%
Elmer Lampe	1938/39	1949/50	12	126	147	273	46.15%										273	126	147	46.15%
Harry Miller	1970/71	1987/88	10	139	131	270	51.48%	1976	1976	1	1	0	1	0.00%			271	139	132	51.29%
Chris Lowery	2004/05	2011/12	8	145	116	261	55.56%	2005	2007	3	6	3	3	50.00%			267	148	119	55.43%
Larry Davis	1997/98	2005/06	9	124	139	263	47.15%										263	124	139	47.15%
Jeff Meyer	1988/89	1996/97	9	134	127	261	51.34%	1994	1994	1	1	0	1	0.00%			262	134	128	51.15%
Tony Barbee	2006/07	2013/14	8	131	127	258	50.78%	2010	2010	1	1	0	1	0.00%			259	131	128	50.58%
Bob Reinhart	1985/86	1993/94	9	107	148	255	41.96%	1991	1991	1	1	0	1	0.00%			256	107	149	41.80%
Greg Graham	2002/03	2009/10	8	142	112	254	55.91%	2008	2008	1	1	0	1	0.00%			255	142	113	55.69%
Kyle Macy	1997/98	2005/06	9	106	144	250	42.40%										250	106	144	42.40%
Harry Good	1943/44	1953/54	11	121	128	249	48.59%										249	121	128	48.59%
Bill Perigo	1949/50	1959/60	11	119	127	246	48.37%										246	119	127	48.37%

Why Indiana is the Center of the Basketball World

SO-NCAA: Career Stats for NCAA Coaches from Indiana

Coach	1st Season	Latest Season	# Years	RS Win	RS Loss	RS GC	RS Win%	1st Tourn	Latest Tourn	# Tourn	Tourn GC	Tourn Win	Tourn Loss	Tourn Win%	Finals	Champ	TOT GC	TOT Win	TOT Loss	TOT Win%
Ralph Jones	1903/04	1919/20	17	194	51	245	79.18%										245	194	51	79.18%
Dave Farrar	1991/92	2000/01	9	110	134	244	45.08%										244	110	134	45.08%
Steve Newton	1985/86	1992/93	8	136	100	236	57.63%	1988	1991	3	4	1	3	25.00%			240	137	103	57.08%
Dave Strack	1959/60	1967/68	9	124	104	228	54.39%	1964	1966	3	10	7	3	70.00%	1		238	131	107	55.04%
Brad Stevens	2007/08	2012/13	6	166	49	215	77.21%	2008	2013	5	17	12	5	70.59%	2		232	178	54	76.72%
Charles Finley	1944/45	1953/54	8	117	109	226	51.77%										226	117	109	51.77%
Zora Clevenger	1904/05	1919/20	15	151	72	223	67.71%										223	151	72	67.71%
Tom Smith	1980/81	1987/88	8	84	138	222	37.84%										222	84	138	37.84%
Bryce Drew	2011/12	2016/17	6	143	65	208	68.75%	2013	2017	3	3	0	3	0.00%			211	143	68	67.77%
Gerry Gerrard	1942/43	1949/50	8	131	78	209	62.68%										209	131	78	62.68%
Bob Stevens	1959/60	1966/67	8	80	124	204	39.22%										204	80	124	39.22%
Pat Knight	2007/08	2013/14	7	79	123	202	39.11%	2012	2012	1	1	0	1	0.00%			203	79	124	38.92%
Norm Ellenberger	1972/73	1978/79	7	134	62	196	68.37%	1974	1978	2	4	2	2	50.00%			200	136	64	68.00%
Richard Crozier	1905/06	1923/24	15	119	81	200	59.50%										200	119	81	59.50%
Larry Steele	1987/88	1993/94	7	56	141	197	28.43%										197	56	141	28.43%
Jay McCreary	1957/58	1964/65	8	82	115	197	41.62%										197	82	115	41.62%
Vern Payne	1982/83	1988/89	7	69	126	195	35.38%										195	69	126	35.38%
Clem Crowe	1933/34	1944/45	11	111	84	195	56.92%										195	111	84	56.92%
Mitch Henderson	2011/12	2016/17	6	119	60	179	66.48%	2017	2017	1	1	0	1	0.00%			180	119	61	66.11%
E.C. Hayes	1911/12	1923/24	12	124	54	178	69.66%										178	124	54	69.66%
Billy Hahn	1986/87	2003/04	6	79	99	178	44.38%										178	79	99	44.38%
Jerry Peirson	1984/85	1989/90	6	94	80	174	54.02%	1985	1986	2	2	0	2	0.00%			176	94	82	53.41%
Ed Schilling	1997/98	2002/03	6	75	93	168	44.64%										168	75	93	44.64%
Glenn Curtis	1938/39	1945/46	8	122	45	167	73.05%										167	122	45	73.05%
Don Smith	1979/80	1984/85	6	84	83	167	50.30%										167	84	83	50.30%
Mel Thompson	1960/61	1966/67	7	67	96	163	41.10%										163	67	96	41.10%
Monte Towne	2001/02	2005/06	5	70	78	148	47.30%										148	70	78	47.30%
Loren Ellis	1941/42	1946/47	6	87	60	147	59.18%										147	87	60	59.18%
Jerry Reynolds	2007/08	2011/12	5	63	82	145	43.45%										145	63	82	43.45%
Al Brown	1982/83	1986/87	5	68	75	143	47.55%	1986	1986	1	1	0	1	0.00%			144	68	76	47.22%
Mark Slessinger	2012/13	2016/17	5	60	83	143	41.96%	2017	2017	1	1	0	1	0.00%			144	60	84	41.67%
Earl Brown	1941/42	1947/48	6	72	70	142	50.70%										142	72	70	50.70%
Scott Hicks	1999/00	2003/04	5	27	114	141	19.15%										141	27	114	19.15%
Alan Major	2010/11	2014/15	5	67	70	137	48.91%										137	67	70	48.91%
Lew Hirt	1946/47	1950/51	5	76	61	137	55.47%										137	76	61	55.47%
Al Harden	1972/73	1976/77	5	61	70	131	46.56%										131	61	70	46.56%
Craig Neal	2013/14	2016/17	4	76	52	128	59.38%	2014	2014	1	1	0	1	0.00%			129	76	53	58.91%
Matthew Graves	2013/14	2016/17	4	51	78	129	39.53%										129	51	78	39.53%
Pete Vaughn	1919/20	1924/25	6	95	34	129	73.64%										129	95	34	73.64%
Bill Harrell	1969/70	1973/74	5	68	59	127	53.54%										127	68	59	53.54%
Lou Watson	1965/66	1970/71	5	62	60	122	50.82%	1967	1967	1	2	1	1	50.00%			124	63	61	50.81%
Dobbie Lambert	1957/58	1961/62	5	61	63	124	49.19%										124	61	63	49.19%
Telfor Mead	1922/23	1934/35	9	77	44	121	63.64%										121	77	44	63.64%
Kirk Earlywine	2007/08	2010/11	4	42	78	120	35.00%										120	42	78	35.00%
Pinky Spruhan	1913/14	1921/22	9	91	25	116	78.45%										116	91	25	78.45%
Dale Waters	1945/46	1952/53	5	38	72	110	34.55%										110	38	72	34.55%
Joe Dean	1989/90	1992/93	4	37	73	110	33.64%										110	37	73	33.64%
John Stroia	1989/90	1992/93	4	29	81	110	26.36%										110	29	81	26.36%
Happy Wann	1915/16	1920/21	5	80	29	109	73.39%										109	80	29	73.39%
Ajac Triplett	1979/80	1982/83	4	44	62	106	41.51%										106	44	62	41.51%
William Spaulding	1913/14	1920/21	8	66	38	104	63.46%										104	66	38	63.46%
John Harmon	1924/25	1934/35	7	64	40	104	61.54%										104	64	40	61.54%
Jack Waters	1973/74	1976/77	4	31	72	103	30.10%										103	31	72	30.10%
Brad Snyder	1968/69	1972/73	5	30	71	101	29.70%										101	30	71	29.70%
John Kimmel	1899/00	1910/11	11	28	72	100	28.00%										100	28	72	28.00%

Printed in the United States
By Bookmasters